I0019998

SQL Server
INTERVIEW QUESTIONS
YOU'LL MOST LIKELY BE ASKED

366
Interview Questions

VIBRANT
PUBLISHERS

SQL Server
Interview Questions
You'll Most Likely Be Asked

ISBN-10: 1-946383-04-X
ISBN-13: 978-1-946383-04-4

Library of Congress Control Number: 2016961100

Vibrant Publishers books are available at special quantity discount for sales promotions, or for use in corporate training programs. For more information please write to **bulkorders@vibrantpublishers.com**

Please email feedback / corrections (technical, grammatical or spelling) to **spellerrors@vibrantpublishers.com**

To access the complete catalogue of Vibrant Publishers, visit **www.vibrantpublishers.com**

Table of Contents

This page is intentionally left blank.

SQL Server Interview

Questions

Review these typical interview questions and think about how you would answer them. Read the answers listed; you will find best possible answers along with strategies and suggestions.

This page is intentionally left blank.

Chapter 1

Engine Enhancements

1: List out the major engine enhancements in SQL Server 2005 database engine.

Answer:

Some of the major engine enhancements featured in SQL Server 2005 are in the fields of Programmability, Manageability, Distributed Queries, Availability, XML, Scalability and Performance, International Enhancements and Security Enhancements. Some major improvements are the introduction of new data types, integration of SQL programming with the .Net environment, the database engine can be managed more dynamically, improved indexing, backup and restore features, XML data type, improved native table and index partitions, improved characterset support and better security enhancements. The latest version, SQL Server 2016, is promising some enhancements in Stretch Database, Foreign Key relationship limits and SERVERPROPERTY. It also has upgrades in the Analysis Services, Master Data Services, Integration Services and Reporting Services.

2: List three major Programmability Enhancements in SQL Server 2005 database engine.

Answer:

Some of the major Programmability enhancements featured in SQL Server 2005 are:

a) New data types like CLR, XML and large object data types such as varchar(max), nvarchar(max) etc.

b) Integration with .Net framework for using T-SQL statements, Triggers, Stored Procedures and User-defined Functions within the Visual Studio IDE. This gives more options in the .Net framework to manipulate and debug database programming easily.

c) New operators in Transact SQL such as APPLY, PIVOT and UNPIVOT. The APPLY operator lets the user call a function that returns a table data type or a subquery against each row of the outer query. PIVOT and UNPIVOT are used to turn the rows into columns and columns into rows (rotating data) for cross-tab reports.

3: List four major Manageability Enhancements in SQL Server 2005 database engine.

Answer:

The main Manageability Enhancements in SQL Server 2005 is that

the database engine can be managed more dynamically. The users and schemas are separated now for better security, table and Index partitioning has improved considerably, files can be initialised instantly and managing the indexes has become easier. The three major enhancements are:

a) **In the Security aspects** – the 2005 release has included a GRANT permission which can be used to grant all permissions. The objects are now stored in schemas and individual users cannot own them. Instead, access is given to specific roles for specific schemas. Users who belong to these roles can access the schema and the objects in it.

b) **For the Administrators** – table and index partitions are allowed in 2005 release. This makes managing bulk data much easier. Dynamic memory management is possible now which supports large databases as against the static memory in the earlier versions which had limitations.

c) **Managing the indexes has become simpler** and more effective in 2005 release. Now the administrators can reorganize, rebuild or disable the indexes easily.

d) Since XML has become a new data type in 2005 version, now we **can create a new XML schema** for storing and managing XML documents within the database.

4: List the major Security Enhancements in SQL Server 2005 database engine.

Answer:

The latest Security enhancements are reduced surface area during installation using a configuration tool, data encryption within the database, granular permission, password policy at par with Windows Server 2003, security context for module execution is defined and multiple proxy accounts are allowed. During installation, all features are not installed by default as earlier. This reduces the surface area required for installation. The Surface Area Configuration tool allows the user to manage the server's external safety profile using a GUI. Module signing lets hiding the inner modules and schema of the database from the end user. The first module which is open to the end user is granted permission and there the basic security validations can be done. SQL Server 2005 allows the stored procedures, triggers (other than DDL triggers), functions and assemblies to be signed or secured.

5: SQL Server offers a fully integrated hybrid solution. Explain.
Answer:
SQL Server offers a variety of hybrid solutions by providing the following options for the enterprise:

a) Deploy applications on non-virtualized environments
b) Deploy applications on private cloud which is an On-premises cloud
c) Deploy applications on public cloud which is an Off-premises cloud
d) Deploy applications on appliances

Also, all the above options can be integrated with each other.

6: What are the features of SQL Server?
Answer:
SQL supports the following features:

a) High Performance

b) Easy to Maintain

c) Scalability

d) Security

e) Availability

f) Easy to Code - Program

7: List the new availability enhancements supported in SQL Server 2012.

Answer:

The new availability enhancements supported in SQL Server 2012 are:

a) AlwaysOn Availability Groups

b) AlwaysOn Failover Cluster Instances

c) Windows Server Core support and

d) Recovery Advisor.

8: What are the features of SQL Server supported in Enterprise Edition?

Answer:

SQL Server supports the following features in enterprise edition:

a) **Data Quality Services:** Technology used to manage and measure data quality

b) **Master Data Services:** To compare external data with master data

c) **Columnstore Indexing:** Performing indexing by storing data in memory

d) Advanced Auditing, Reporting, and Analytics

e) Partitioning and Compression

f) **TDE:** Transparent Data Encryption

g) Advanced High Availability achieved with AlwaysOn feature

h) Supports all Business Intelligence Edition feature

9: What are the features of SQL Server supported in Business Intelligence Edition?

Answer:

SQL supports the following features in Business Intelligence edition:

a) Supports a maximum of 16 cores for DB (Database) engine

b) High Availability achieved with AlwaysOn 2 Node failover clusters

c) Multidimensional BI (Business Intelligence) semantic model

d) Power View, Analytics, and Reporting

e) Spatial Support, File table, and policy based management

10: How do availability enhancements support for Windows server core?

Answer:

Windows server core is a scaled down edition of Windows OS (Operating System), and it requires fewer reboots (approximately 50-60%) when patching servers leading to higher server uptime and increased security.

11: What is the benefit of Recovery Advisor?

Answer:

The Recovery Advisor provides a Visual timeline to simplify the DB restore process. The timeline is used mainly to specify the backups and restore database at a specific point of time.

12: What are the scalability and performance enhancements available in SQL Server?

Answer:

The following are the scalability and performance enhancements features of SQL Server which allows to improve the server workloads:

a) Column Store Indexes

b) Higher partition support

c) Online Indexing

d) Achieve maximum scalability using Windows Server 2008 R2

13: What are the Manageability Enhancements of SQL Server 2012?

Answer:

The following are the Manageability Enhancement features of SQL Server 2012:

a) Management Studio

b) Transact-SQL Debugger

c) IntelliSense Enhancements

d) Insert Snippet Menu and

e) Resource Governor enhancements

f) Contained databases

g) Tight integration with SQL Azure

h) Data-Tier Application (DAC) Enhancements

14: What are the security enhancements of SQL Server?

Answer:

The security capabilities and controls of SQL Server are:

a) Provides user-defined roles for easily allocating the responsibilities

b) Improve compliance and resiliency, it provides audit enhancements

c) Provides default schema for Groups

d) Contained Database Authentication provides DB authentication that uses self-contained access information without the need for server logins

e) Share point and Active directory security model for higher data security in end-user reports

15: What are the programmability enhancements of SQL Server?

Answer:

For programmability enhancements, SQL Server provides support for the following data types:

a) XML

b) Digital Media

c) Spatial Documents

d) Scientific Records

e) Factoids

f) Other unstructured data types

16: Explain DAC enhancements.

Answer:

DAC refers to Data tier Application. This is a concept introduced in SQL Server 2008 R2. It is a single unit of deployment containing database's schema, dependent objects and deployment requirements used by an application. The enhancements for DAC 2012 are:

a) Upgrades are performed in an in-place fashion instead of the side-by-side upgrade process that existed for years

b) DAC could be deployed, imported and exported across enterprise and in public cloud such as SQL Azure

c) DAC support many more objects compared to the previous version

17: Explain how SQL Server supports tight integration with SQL Azure.

Answer:

This is one of the manageability enhancement supports of SQL Server. SQL Server provides an interface for deploying a new database to SQL Azure through which the enterprise can deploy an on-premise database to SQL Azure. Also, new cloud services are enabled and available in SQL Azure data sync which provides bidirectional data synchronization between databases across the data center and cloud.

18: Explain Resource Governor Enhancements.

Answer:

Resource Governor Enhancement is a manageability enhancement of SQL Server. The important benefits are:

a)   It is used for the management of workloads and resources by implementing limits on the consumption of resources based on incoming requests

b)   The number of resource pools support increased from 24 to 60 in resource governor to meet customer expectations of large resource pool and large scale multitenant database solution with a higher level of isolation between workloads

c)   It has a new DMV (Dynamic Management View) called sys.dm_resource_governor_resource_pool_affinity which improves the DB admin's success in tracking the resource pool affinity

19: Explain Columnstore Index.

Answer:

Columnstore index is introduced in SQL Server 2012. It is an in-memory index build directly in the engine. This is mainly used for performance improvements to improve the queries associated with the data warehouse workloads by 10 to 100 times.

20: Explain the partition support enhancements in SQL Server.

Answer:

SQL Server 2012, by default, supports up to 15,000 partitions per table. This is mainly to boost scalability and performance of large tables and data warehouses. The previous version, by default, supports only 1000 partitions. This increase in partition support helps to enable large sliding-window scenarios for data ware house maintenance.

21: How can SQL Server achieve maximum scalability?

Answer:

SQL Server achieves maximum scalability with the help of Windows Server 2008 R2. This server is mainly build to achieve dynamic scalability, reliability, unprecedented work load size, and across the board availability. Also, Windows Server supports up to 256 logical processors and 2 terra bytes of memory in a single OS instance.

22: What are the additional features included in SQL Server Management Studio?

Answer:

These two features are included in SQL Server 2012 Management Studio:

a) **IntelliSense Enhancements -** IntelliSense Enhancement suggests string matches based on partial words. In the previous version, recommendations were provided based on first character.

b) **Transact-SQL Debugger -** Transact-SQL debugger is used to enhance break point functionality and to debug scripts on the instances of SQL Server versions starting from 2005.

23: What is the use of Contained Databases?

Answer:

The risk associated with the DB is that if the DB is moved to another instance of SQL Server, the login does not exist. This is resolved by Contained DBs, in which users are authenticated directly into DB without need for logins in the DB engine. This feature provides better portability of user DBs among servers because they have no external dependencies.

24: What is the use of FileTable?

Answer:

File Table is a new feature introduced in SQL Server 2012 mainly used to store unstructured data such as media files, XML, and documents which usually reside on a file server. File Table provides namespace support and application compatibility with the data stored in SQL Server. As a result, full text and semantic search is achievable over structured and unstructured data.

25: Explain Full Text search enhancement.

Answer:

Full text search offers better scale and performance in SQL Server 2012. It has property scoped search functionality which allows enterprise to search properties such as Author and title without the need for programmers to have a separate file properties in DB. Programmers benefit by customizing proximity search using NEAR operator that allows specifying the maximum number of non-search terms that separate the first and last terms in a search.

26: What are the editions of SQL Server 2012?

Answer:

SQL Server 2012 has three editions. They are:

    a)   Standard Edition

b) Business Intelligence Edition

c) Enterprise Edition

27: What is an in-place upgrade?

Answer:

The In-Place upgrade replaces the previous versions of binaries to SQL Server 2012 binaries on the existing machine. The data is automatically converted from the previous version to SQL Server 2012. The supported up gradation versions are available from 2005. Upgrading from 2000, 7.0, 6.5 are not supported.

28: What are the benefits of side-by-side migration over an in-place upgrade?

Answer:

Side-by-side migration builds a new DB infrastructure on SQL Server 2012 and avoids migration issues that might occur with an in-place upgrade. It also provides more control over the upgrade progress and can migrate DB and component independently. Performing a rollback is easy when performing the migration.

29: What are the high level steps performed for Step-by-Step migration?

Answer:

The following are the high level migration steps for upgrading to SQL Server 2012:

a) Ensure the instance of SQL Server meets the software and hardware requirements

b) Review the discontinued and deprecated features

c) Be sure to run the 2012 Upgrade Advisor to migrate the

data and verify it proceeds smoothly

d) Procure the hardware and install Windows Server 2012 (highly recommended)

e) Install the SQL Server 2012 prerequisites and desired components

f) Migrate objects from legacy server to new DB platform

g) Point applications to the new DB

h) Ensure the legacy servers are decommissioned after the migration is complete

30: What are the advantages of In-Place upgrade in SQL Server?
Answer:
Following are the advantages of in-place upgrade in SQL Server:

a) The strategy followed in in-place upgrade is less risky and easy to upgrade

b) The in-place upgrade process is very fast and it does not require any supporting hardware

c) During the upgrade process, the server instance names never get changed

d) The in-place upgrade is less time consuming as it does not require making changes in the application connection properties

Chapter 2

Availability and Disaster Recovery Enhancements

31: Explain the Availability modes supported by SQL Server.

Answer:

SQL Server supports two Availability modes –

    a) Synchronous Commit Mode and

    b) Asynchronous Commit Mode

The Synchronous Commit Mode keeps a synchronous commit primary replica and synchronous commit secondary replica ready before the actual commit is made. The primary replica ensures that the secondary replica has completed writing the committed records to the database log before the SQL commits a transaction. The secondary database is synchronised to the primary database under this mode which ensures that the transactions committed are protected. The only issue here is the increased time taken for completing the transaction.

The Asynchronous Commit Mode does not wait for the database replica log to be updated. Here the transaction may be completed faster but the data that is committed is not protected. Under the Asynchronous commit mode, there are more chances of losing some or most part of the committed data.

32: What do you know about the Always On Availability Groups in SQL Server?
Answer:
The Always On Availability groups were added to the SQL Server Enterprise Edition 2012. The basic concept here is to maintain 1 primary database replica and up to 4 secondary database replicas of the primary database. These replicas are concurrently accessed by the Enterprise users who may be trying to commit transactions to the same SQL logs. To make sure that none of them fail, each transaction is provided a separate set of database replicas which are known as the Availability Groups. These replicas can also be used to display data in reports or for taking backups. All 5 availability groups are allowed read-write access to the database. One main characteristic of the availability group is that they fail over together. The Always On availability mode is a property of the availability group which makes sure that the user database is available to be accessed by the enterprise user to the maximum. The Always On Availability mode supports Synchronous and

Asynchronous commit modes.

33: Explain Failover in AlwaysOn.

Answer:

Failover is the process where the synchronising primary and secondary database replicas switch their roles according to availability. If during a transaction, the primary database replica fails to commit, the secondary replica takes over as the primary replica and continues with the transaction. When the actual primary replica recovers it automatically becomes a secondary to the now primary replica and continues the synchronization process. Failover exists in 3 forms – automatic, manual and forced where the chances of data loss is maximum. The types of failover supported depends on the availability mode. The synchronous commit mode supports planned manual failover and automatic failover. In both the cases, the chances of data loss is very less. The asynchronous commit mode supports only forced failover where the chances of data loss is high.

34: How do you design a backup and recovery solution to the SQL Server database?

Answer:

The following steps can lead to a decent backup and recovery plan.

First, we need to establish 'What is Needed?'. Based on what is actually needed, the recovery model has to be established. Then the backup type has to be determined. Backup can be done in full, selective or partial mode, it can be a file or filegroup backup, copy-only backup, transaction log backup or mirror backup. Once the appropriate backup type is selected, the backup schedule is planned and the backup process can be carried out. The backups need to be documented to keep track. The primary backup can be to the Disk and then archived to the Tape. Make sure to backup to Different Drives or else if the system crashes, the running database as well as the backups will be lost. Secure the Backup Files with encryption or passwords to make sure it is not accessed by unauthorised parties. It is also necessary to compress the Backup Files so that it does not eat away the precious hard disk space. How much to keep on the disk and how much online is another factor to consider. Verify the backups with Restore Verifyonly command to make sure the backups are not corrupted and can be used later to restore. An Offsite Storage for the backup is highly desirable to ensure its availability in case of a disaster.

35: What is the strategy used for high availability and disaster recovery with SQL server versions prior to 2012?

Answer:

The following two strategies were used for high availability and disaster recovery in the older versions of SQL Server:

a) Asynchronous data base mirroring for disaster recovery for mission-critical databases

b) Failover clustering within the data center combined with log shipping to protect SQL Server instances and moving data to multiple locations

36: What is the issue with Database mirroring?

Answer:

Database mirroring is a good way to protect databases, but the solution is a one-to-one mapping, making multiple secondaries (multiple instances of SQL Server) unattainable. So, in order to have multiple secondaries, enterprises choose log shipping over database mirroring.

37: What is the issue with Log shipping?

Answer:

The limitation or issue with log shipping is that it does not provide zero data loss or automatic fail over capability since this requires transferring the machine to the deployment destination.

38: What are the new features for high availability and disaster recovery introduced in SQL Server 2012?

Answer:

In SQL Server 2012, there are two new features introduced for high availability and disaster recovery. They are:

a) **AlwaysOn Availability Groups:** This feature supports DB protection and failover

b) **AlwaysOn Failover Cluster Instances:** This feature to supports DB protection at instance level and multi-site clustering

39: What are the high level benefits of AlwaysOn Availability Groups?

Answer:

The high level benefits of AlwaysOn Availability Groups are:

a) **DB protection:** Provides zero data loss thereby protecting the database

b) **Multi DB failover:** Provides automatic or manual failover for a group of databases

c) **Multiple secondaries:** Units or clusters in which failover support is provided for up to 4 secondaries

d) **Integrated HA management:** HA refers to High Availability which helps enterprise to make data available all the time

40: What are the high level benefits of AlwaysOn Failover Cluster Instances?

Answer:

The high level benefits of AlwaysOn Failover Cluster Instances are:

a) **Instance level protection:** Provides protection on SQL server instance level thereby supports zero data loss

b) **Multisite clustering:** Provides clustering support for multiple sites

c) **Consolidation:** This option helps to replicate data between different storage systems i.e., from one node to another node

41: What is the benefit of synchronous and asynchronous data movement in AlwaysOn Availability Groups?

Answer:

In AlwaysOn Availability Groups, Synchronous data movement is used to provide high availability within the primary data center.

In AlwaysOn Availability Groups, Asynchronous data movement is used to provide disaster recovery.

42: What steps should be followed while deploying AlwaysOn Availability Groups?

Answer:

The below steps are performed when deploying the AlwaysOn Availability Groups:

a) Deploy Windows failover cluster using Failover cluster manager snap-in

b) Perform the configuration step in SQL Server management studio which automatically creates the services, application, and resources in Failover cluster manager

The deployment is very easy for DB administrators who are not familiar with failover clustering.

43: What are the features in AlwaysOn Availability Groups?

Answer:

AlwaysOn Availability has the following new concepts or features:

a) **Availability Replica Roles:** This feature provides failover coordination, distributed change notification, and primary health detection

b) **Data synchronization modes:** This moves data from primary replica to secondary replica synchronously or asynchronously

c) **Failover modes:** This provides support for both manual and automatic failover

d) **Connection mode in secondaries:** This provides support for connections, or disallows connections, or allows read-only connections

e) **Availability Group Listeners:** This provides the option to connect to databases within virtual networks

44: What are Active Secondaries?

Answer:

Active Secondaries are secondary replicas which provide read-only access to databases that are affiliated with an availability group. In the active secondaries, all the read-only operations are supported by row versioning and are automatically mapped to support transaction.

45: What are the benefits of secondaries in AlwaysOn Availability Groups?

Answer:

The following are the benefits of secondaries in AlwaysOn Availability Groups:

a) Efficiency is improved

b) Performance is increased

c) Reduction in total cost with better resource utilization

d) Leveraged for backups and read-only operations such as reporting and maintenance

46: What are the connection modes available in secondaries?

Answer:

The three connection modes available in secondaries are:

a) **Disallow connection:** This replica does not allow any connection

b) **Allow only read-intent connections:** This replica allows only read-intent connections

c) **Allow all:** This replica allows all connections for read access including connections running with older clients

47: What are the failover modes in Availability Groups?

Answer:

There are two failover modes for the DB administrators to choose from while configuring AlwaysOn Availability Groups. They are:

a) **Automatic failover mode:** This replica uses the synchronous commit availability mode and supports both manual and automatic failover between replica partners. It supports a maximum of 2 failover replica partners when choosing automatic failover

b) **Manual failover mode:** This replica uses either the synchronous or the asynchronous commit availability mode. This mode supports only manual failovers between replica partners

48: What is the availability group listener?

Answer:

The availability group listener is a feature in "AlwaysOn Availability groups" which provides an option to connect to databases through virtual private networks. This concept is similar to Virtual SQL Server which is created while using failover clustering.

49: How will you configure availability group listener?

Answer:

We can configure availability group listener in two ways. They are:

a) In SQL Server Management Studio we can specify the availability group listener in the "Create a New Availability Group" window

b) We can use Transact-SQL to create or modify the listener

For both modes, configuring the availability group listener requires a DNS name, an IP address, and a port number.

50: What are the deployment configuration steps for HA and DR requirements?

Answer:

The diagram below shows the deployment configuration steps to be performed for High Availability (HA) and Disaster Recovery (DR) requirements, while configuring the New Availability Group in SQL Server Management Studio:

a) Specify the SQL server instance name in the 'Server Instance' column

b) Specify if it is a Primary or Secondary replica in the 'Initial Role' column

c) Specify which instance you want to choose for Automatic Fail Over in the 'Automatic Failover (Up to 2)' column

d) Specify which instance you choose for synchronous commit in the 'Synchronous Commit (Up to 3)' column

e) Specify which instance is readable in 'Readable Secondary' column

51: What are the deployment alternatives for Disaster Recovery?
Answer:

The following are the deployment alternatives for Disaster
Recovery:

a) Make the SQL Server instance as non-shared storage and
create separate instances in local, Regional and for Geo-
Target

b) Create a multi-site cluster with another cluster as Disaster
Recovery Target

c) Create a three-node (3 instance) cluster with similar
Disaster Recovery Target

d) Create secondary targets for Backup, Reporting, and
Disaster Recovery

52: How are availability groups monitored in SQL Server 2012?
Answer:

In SQL Server 2012, administrators are provided with an intuitive
manageability dashboard to monitor availability groups. The
dashboard is launched by right-clicking the Availability Groups
folder in the Object Explorer in SQL Server Management Studio
and selecting 'Show Dashboard' option.

53: What is monitored with the availability groups' dashboard?
Answer:

The following can be monitored with the availability group's
dashboard:

a) Health and status of the SQL Server instance

b) The availability database in the availability group

c) The specific replica (SQL Server instance) role and provide
the status to stakeholders

In the dashboard, the database administrator can look for additional information like availability group state, server instance name, and health status by clicking on the respective headings in the dashboard.

54: What are the features of AlwaysOn Failover Cluster Instances?

Answer:

These are the features of AlwaysOn Failover Cluster Instances:

a) **Multi subnet Clustering:** This provides a disaster-recovery solution in addition to high availability with new support for multi-subnet failover clustering

b) **Support for TempDB on local disk:** This provides storage within the local server nodes to optimize TempDB workloads

c) **Flexible failover policy:** This provides the failure condition properties that allow the configuration of a more flexible failover policy

55: Name all operating systems that support installation of SQL Server 2012.

Answer:

The following Operating Systems support installation of SQL Server 2012:

a) Windows Server 2008 R2 Service Package 1 Web Server Core

b) Windows Server 2008 R2 Service Package 1 Standard Server Core

c) Windows Server 2008 R2 Service Package 1 Enterprise
   Server Core

d) Windows Server 2008 R2 Service Package 1 Data Center
   Server Core

All of the above operating systems support only in 64 bit system.

56: What are the prerequisites for installing SQL Server 2012 on Windows Server 2008?

Answer:

The following are the prerequisites for installing SQL Server 2012
in Windows Server 2008:

a) .NET Framework 2.0 SP2

b) .NET Framework 3.5 SP1 Full Profile

c) .NET Framework 4 Server Core Profile

d) Windows Installer 4.5

e) Windows PowerShell 2.0

All the above components must be installed before installing SQL
Server 2012 on Windows Server 2008.

57: What SQL Server features are supported on Server Core?

Answer:

The following SQL Server features are supported on Server Core:

a) **Database Engine Services:** This supports monitoring the
   data flow, back up frequency, and cluster node details

b) **SQL Server Replication:** This supports replication in
   multiple instances

c) **Full Text search:** This provides search for text with limited
   characters followed by delimiters

d) **Analysis Services:** This supports analysis of configuring multi-site clusters in SQL Server instances

e) **Client tools connectivity:** This supports connectivity to multiple clusters across instances

f) **Integration Services:** This supports replicating data in more than one instance and there by avoid data loss

58: What is Database Recovery Advisor?

Answer:

The Database Recovery Advisor is a new feature introduced in SQL Server 2012. This option allows the database administrators to conduct database recovery tasks. This advisor provides a wizard so database administrators can visualize the backup history and restoration time line in a User Interface.

This page is intentionally left blank.

Chapter 3

Columnstore Index

59: Explain Columnstore Index in SQL Server.

Answer:

Typically, a relational database like SQL Server stores the data row-wise or column-wise in a page. In the row-wise storage, multiple rows are stored in a page. In the column-wise index, each column with multiple rows are stored in a page. This makes a query on a particular column easier to fetch. Columnstore index helps in reports and views where data is consolidated based on a column. Columnstore index is very useful in data analytics and data warehousing. We can mention the type of index to be applied to a table after the table is created. The following SQL command is used to create a columnstore index for a table:

CREATE COLUMNSTORE <ColumnStoreIndex name> ON <TableName> (<Columnname1>, <ColumnName2>, .. <ColumnNameN>)

60: What are the disadvantages of Columnstore Index in SQL Server?

Answer:

Columnstore Indices were actually created for OLAP processes to improve the performance of select statements. This resulted in certain drawbacks such as:

a) You cannot insert, update, delete or merge the records of a colmn store indexed table except if it has a clustered columnstore index.

b) It does not support binary, varbinary, BLOB, CLR, varchar(max), datetimeoffset with accuracy higher than 2 and decimals with more than 18 digits.

c) Cannot apply indexed views

d) Cannot implement replication

e) A table can have only one clustered columstore index though there is no limit on the size.

f) Since each column index is stored in a different page, a query involving more than one column takes longer to fetch the corresponding records from different pages.

61: Explain Clustered and Non-Clustered Columnstore Indexes.

Answer:

A Clustered Columnstore Index is the physical storage of the table and will be the only columnstore index of the table. A Clustered Columnstore Index allows insert, update and delete operations on the table and will also allow data bulk-load into the table. A Clustered Columnstore Index uses a temporary rowstore table called a deltastore which contains the rows of the table till the data gets large enough to be moved to a columnstore.

Non-Clustered Columnstore Indexes are read-only indexes of the table. A table can have any number of Non-Clustered Columnstore Indexes which are used for reporting and data analytics. Non-Clustered Columnstore Index contains a read-only copy of the table which can be used for any read-only operation involving the table.

62: How does a columnstore index achieve fast query performance?

Answer:

Columnstore Index helps you to achieve upto 10 times better data compression and upto 100 times better query performance for data warehousing. Columnstore indexes achieve this by a blend of rapid batch-wise in-memory processing methods that reduce IO requisites. Analytics queries require a large number of rows to be fetched into the memory for processing. Since this involves a large volume of IO, other IO requirements are avoided. Similarly, once this this large volume of data enters the memory, the in-memory operations also are curbed. These reduced IO and optimization of in-memory processes are attained through data compression, eliminating the columnstore, eliminating the rowstore and executing batch processing. Data compression is achieved by storing and retrieving compressed data for in-memory processing. Since data is stored columnwise similar data type only have to be considered which further enhances data compression. Eliminating the column is possible since data is stored column-wise. Eliminating the row is made possible as the columnstore index fetches only the matched records for the fetch query given by the metadata without actually performing any IO. Columnstore index always performs batch execution which usually takes upto 900 rows in each batch. This increases the efficiency and spreads the query cost to the batches rather than the rows.

63: What is the new index type introduced in SQL Server 2012?
Answer:
The new index type introduced in SQL Server 2012 is called 'columnstore'. During the development phase and during the distribution release (Community Technology Preview) of SQL Server 2012, this index type 'columnstore' is initially referred as Project Apollo.

64: What is the most important benefit of columnstore index?
Answer:
The most important benefit of columnstore index is that it provides the database administrators advanced query processing enhancements which have drastically increased the query performance for the data warehouse workloads. The improvement of query performance is by 10 to 100 times than the previous performance (when columnstore index is not in use).

65: How many columnstore indexes can be created for a table?
Explain with an example.
Answer:
Only one columnstore index can be created for a particular table as shown below:

CREATE COLUMNSTORE INDEX testindex ON testtable
(column1, column3, column4);

The above query will create the columnstore index called
'testindex' for the table 'testtable' on the columns column1,
column3, and column4.

66: How is data stored in a database using columnstore index?

Answer:

Prior to columnstore index, data in SQL Server is stored in a row-
based fashion. This storage model is called as row store. Using
columnstore index, the data is stored in each column, which is
available in a separate set of disk pages instead of storing data in
multiple rows per page. Also, the data stored in the column
always exists in a compressed form.

67: What data types are supported by columnstore index?

Answer:

The following data types are supported by columnstore index:

a) **int, smallint, bigint:** Iinteger data types used to store
   whole numbers

b) **char, varchar:** Character data types used to store text
   values

c) **real, float:** Decimal data types used to store real value in
   decimals

d) **string:** Used to store string values

e) **money, smallmoney:** Used to store values in money
   format

f) **date and time:** Used to store date and time

68: How does data appear in the table when you use columnstore format?

Answer:

The data in SQL Server appears as below when you use columnstore format:

USERID	101	102	103
NAME	Jose	Allan	Cook
PINCODE	55047	42035	21183

In the above table, the data appears in a column-wise format rather than the typical row format.

69: What data types are not supported by columnstore index?

Answer:

The following data types are not supported in the columnstore index:

a) **BLOB (Binary Large Objects):** This refers to any file (Ex: image, document, PDF, etc)

b) **(n) varchar (max):** This refers to unspecified character types

c) **binary, varbinary:** This refers to binary which is represented as 0 and 1

d) Decimal types that are greater than 18 digits

e) **CLR:** This denotes the in-build SQL Server data type hierarchy id

70: How does columnstore index improve the query speed?

Answer:

The columnstore index improves the query speed by using the following approach:

   a) Columnstore index uses VertiPaq compression algorithm with which column data is compressed and high level compression of data can be achieved

   b) With columnstore index, less space is required to store data in memory. Because of this, data transfer from disk to memory is reduced which improves the query speed.

71: Explain Batch-mode processing.

Answer:

Batch-mode processing is an advanced technology used to process queries that retrieve columnstore index data.

The column data is processed in batches using the vector technology that is highly efficient which works well with columnstore index. This batch-mode processing utilizes Hash Join and Hash Aggregation algorithm which optimizes the hardware architecture and improves parallelism.

72: Explain about segments in columnstore index.

Answer:

In columnstore index, the data is broken into segments. For example:

SEGMENT			
Column 1	Column 2	Column 3	Column 4

ROWGROUP

Each column data is a segment which contains data up to 1 million rows. Each row is called a row group. Each segment is stored internally in a LOB (Large Object). So, when SQL Server reads data, each segment processes data between disk and memory.

73: What are the restrictions in columnstore index?

Answer:

The restrictions in columnstore index are:

a) Can't enable PAGE compression or row compression in columnstore index but only in the base table

b) If tables and its columns use 'Change data capture' (To monitor if data has been modified), then it is not possible to use columnstore index

c) If columnstore index is applied on a table, then data replication over server is not possible

d) Columnstore index can't be created on indexed view

74: Which statements are not allowed when you use columnstore index?

Answer:

When columnstore index is created for a table, then insert, merge, delete and update statements cannot be used.

For example:

Assume that columnstore index is created on 'testtable' using the below query

    CREATE COLUMNSTORE INDEX testindex ON testtable
    (column1, column3, column4);

For the above table 'testtable', insert, delete, merge, and update queries cannot be used.

75: When should a columnstore index be created?

Answer:

The columnstore index has to be created for the following scenarios:

a) To store read-only data (warehouse data)

b) To handle new data which requires partitioning (splitting data and storing it in multiple columns)

c) To aggregate and large volume of data

For the above mentioned scenarios, creating a columnstore index will optimize the performance.

76: When should a columnstore index not be created?

Answer:

A columnstore index should not be created in the following scenarios:

a) If the data changes frequently

b) If the partition does not meet the workflow (Example: processing a bank account for an account holder) requirement of your enterprise

For the above scenarios, B-Tree index performs better than columnstore index.

77: What are the options for loading new data in a columnstore index table?

Answer:

There are three options for loading new data in a columnstore index table:

a) **Disable columnstore index:** Update data and rebuild index when the data is completed

b) **Leverage Partitioning:** This enables database administrators to access and manage subsets of columnstore index data quickly and efficiently

c) **Union All:** Using this option, Database administrators can load data by storing main data in a fact table that has columnstore and create a secondary table to update or add data

78: How is new data loaded by using partitioning?
Answer:

By using partitioning, load new data by performing the below three steps:

a) To accept new data, make sure you have an empty partition in the server

b) Then load the data into the empty staging table

c) Then switch the staging table that contains the newly loaded data into the empty partition

79: How is existing data updated by using partitioning?
Answer:

By using partitioning update existing data by performing the below steps:

a) First identify which partition contains the data that needs to be modified

b) Next switch the partition into the empty staging table

c) Then on the staging table, disable the columnstore index

d) The existing data has to be updated

e) Once data updating is complete, rebuild the index on the

staging table

f) Finally, we have to switch the staging table to the original partition

80: What tools are used to create columnstore index?

Answer:

Use one of the following to create columnstore index:

a) **SQL Server Management Studio:** This provides a User Interface to easily configure the columns to be indexed for a particular table

b) **Transact-SQL:** In this approach use the SQL queries to create columnstore index on a particular table

81: Explain the steps to be performed to create columnstore index using Management Studio.

Answer:

Using Management Studio, perform the following steps to create columnstore index:

a) In Management Studio, use object explorer to connect to the SQL Server database instance

b) Next select the table to create columnstore index

c) Then right-click the index folder, choose new index and click non-clustered columnstore index

d) Now type a name for the new index and click 'Add'

e) Finally select the columns to participate in columnstore index and click OK

Performing the above steps will create the columnstore index on the selected columns.

82: How is a clustered columnstore index created?

Answer:

It is not possible to create a clustered columnstore index. Only a non-clustered columnstore index can be created as below:

```
CREATE NONCLUSTERED COLUMNSTORE INDEX
testindex ON testtable (column1, column3, column4);
```

"Non-clustered" indicates that the index is a secondary representation of data.

83: How many columns in a table are supported for columnstore index?

Answer:

Each table supports a maximum of 1024 columns that can be added to the columnstore index. This is one of the restrictions of columnstore index to achieve maximum performance.

84: Write a query that will force ignore the columnstore index.

Answer:

The below query will force ignore the columnstore index for a particular column:

```
Select distinct(MyColumn) from MyTable
    Option(ignore_nonclustered_columnstore_index)
GO
```

In the above query, the column 'MyColumn' will be ignored from indexing from the table 'MyTable'.

85: Write a query that will manually trigger a particular columnstore index.

Answer:

The below query will manually trigger the particular columnstore index:

> Select distinct(MyColumn) from MyTable
>> WITH INDEX (MYNON-CLUSTEREDINDEX)
>> GO

In the above query, the columnstore index "MYNON-CLUSTEREDINDEX" is triggered manually when the above query is executed.

86: Is it possible to have a clustered B-tree index and non-clustered columnstore index in a table? If so, how will the clustered index be queried?

Answer:

It is possible to have a clustered B-tree index and a non-clustered columnstore index in a particular table.

The below query will manually trigger the particular clustered index:

> Select distinct(MyColumn) from MyTable
>> WITH INDEX (MYCLUSTEREDINDEX)
>> GO

In the above query, the clustered index "MYCLUSTEREDINDEX" is triggered manually when the above query is executed.

87: What are the best practices to be followed using columnstore index?

Answer:

The following best practices have to be followed while using columnstore index:

a) Use join queries to attain optimal performance on the search results

b) Avoid Unions, Outer joins, and Union All on columnstore index

c) Always calculate the size of the memory available and memory required since creating columnstore index requires a considerable amount of memory

d) Using batch-mode processing to speed up queries and provide better results

e) Table partitioning has to be considered to update data

f) Use integer data types as they provide compact representation and opportunity for filtering data

Chapter 4

Security Enhancements

88: Explain the Guest User Account in SQL Server.

Answer:

The Guest User is a default user of all databases in SQL Server. Unless explicitly blocked, the Guest User can access every database. For security reasons, it will be better to block the user from accessing application-specific data explicitly. Though it is not mapped to any login, the Guest User can be used by any or all logins. We cannot eliminate the Guest User as it is required for accessing certain system databases like TempDB and Master. Specific application databases may not required the Guest User and hence can be restricted from accessing sensitive data instead of dropping from the DB.

89: Explain the BUILTIN/Administrators Group in SQL Server. What happens when I drop the BUILTIN/Administrators Group?

Answer:

The Windows Login is a default SQL server administrator. This is the builtin Administrator group who can access the database from the Windows login as well as the SQL server login. One major issue with the BuiltIn/Administrator group is that any windows user can access the SQL Server database which is a security threat to sensitive application data. Another issue with this group is that if the windows login is compromised, it can be used to access the SQL Server as an administrator. For security reasons, the BUILTIN/Administrators Group can be deleted after making sure that the sa password is known to the administrator and that the builtin Administrator does not own any database, table or procedure. If required additional logins can be created with specific rights and the existing logins are checked and revoked unnecessary rights. At least one other login needs to have the SQL Server System Administrator rights or you should know the sa password.

90: Explain SQL Injection. How can it be handled and prevented?

Answer:

SQL Injection is the term used when unknown SQL commands are accessing the database to view and / or update the data in a malicious way. SQL Injection requires a 4 step process for identification, analysis, recovery of any data lost and then

prevention of further attacks. Identifying the problem is the basic
issue. It sometimes takes a while before the attack is identified. By
the time some data might be stolen, lost or corrupted. Once the
issue has been identified, the firewall logs, IIS logs, web pages and
the SQL server tables need to be analysed to identify from where
it is being accessed. Another option is to use a performance
monitoring tool that checked for long running SQL statements
which are usually malicious. Now that the issue has been
identified, data recovery is the next step. Depending on whether
data is lost or added need to be determined first. If some malicious
or junk data is added to the system and it has been identified, the
SQL DBA can run a procedure to delete the same. Otherwise the
date of attack has to be identified and the appropriate recovery
has to be done. This will take longer depending on the details of
SQL Injection available. To prevent future attacks the DBA has to
take some strict action for validation of commands and data types
that access the database from the front end, use stored procedures
instead of raw SQL commands, remove unused webpages,
prevent any command from executing some identified bulk
updators like Exec, Cast etc. and use functions in the front end for
any filtering of special characters from the input data. The
Network Administrator also has to make sure unauthorised users
or websites do no access the database.

91: How can you enforce security in SQL Server?
Answer:
The SQL Server DBA can enforce security to the database by
making strong passwords, not allowing too many sysadmins and

creating and assigning specific roles for accessing specific data. Other than that, the SQL Server has some built-in security features such as Data encryption, Password policies, Limited visibility of metadata, User and schema separation, DDL triggers, security catalog views, granular permission sets and duplication. Apart from these, the DBA can take some additional security measures such as revoking the permissions granted to the public database role, using views or stored procedures to access data instead of revealing the tables, disabling network shared on SQL Server, hindering the Guest User, adopting the latest security techniques and updates for SQL Server etc.

92: What were the improvements introduced in SQL Server 2012 for maximum security and control of DB?

Answer:

The following are the SQL Server 2012 improvements for maximum security and control of DB:

   a)   Security Manageability improvements
   b)   Audit enhancements
   c)   Database authentication enhancement
   d)   Crypto Changes
   e)   Miscellaneous security enhancements

93: What were the security manageability improvements introduced with SQL Server 2012?

Answer:

The following security manageability improvements were introduced with SQL Server 2012:

a) 'Default schema for Groups' - a security feature request from SQL community

b) User-defined server roles

94: What is the primary benefit of user-defined server roles?

Answer:

The main benefit of user-defined server roles is to limit system access for only authorized users to reduce security threats, compromised security, and operational mistakes; improving the manageability of users and their privileges.

Use these three steps to implement a user defined server role:

a) Create a server role

b) Specify permissions to the roles

c) Assign new or registered members to the roles

95: What are the available approaches to creating server roles in SQL Server?

Answer:

Use SQL Server Management Studio (SSMS) to create server roles, apply permissions, and add members to the new roles. Transact-SQL statements are also used to create server roles, apply permissions, and add members to roles.

96: What are the steps required to create server roles in SSMS?

Answer:

Follow these steps to create server roles in SSMS:

a) In SQL Server Management Studio, use Object Explorer to connect to an instance of SQL Server DB engine

b) Expand the security folder

c) Right-click server the roles folder and select New Server Role

d) In the New Server Role wizard:

   i)   Enter the name of the new server role

   ii) Select the owner for the new server role

   iii) Choose appropriate securable for the new server role

   iv) Apply one explicit permission (Grant - With Grant - Deny)

e) On the member page, add member logins to represent an individual or groups that are added to the server roles

97: How will you create server roles using Transact-SQL?

Answer:

The following example demonstrates how to create server role using Transact-SQL queries:

```
USE [master];

CREATE SERVER ROLE [DBAMyControlServer]
AUTHORIZATION [sysadmin];

ALTER SERVER ROLE [DBAMyControlServer] ADD
MEMBER [PROTOTYPE\Finance];

GRANT CONTROL SERVER TO [DBAMyControlServer];
GO;


GRANT CREATE DATABASE TO [DBAMyControlServer];
GRANT CREATE AVAILABILITY GROUP TO
[DBAMyControlServer];
```

DENY ALTER LOGIN TO [DBAMyControlServer];

DENY ALTER SERVER AUDIT TO [DBAMyControlServer];

GO;

The above example creates the server role 'DBAControlServer' and applies the security permission for the specific role.

98: How will you define schema?

Answer:

Schema is a meta-data collection that describes the database relations. It explains the way data is organized in the database tables. In other words, it is the structure represented in the Database Management System (DBMS) using a query language the DBMS supports.

In a relational DB, the schema defines the tables, views, indexes, fields, relationships, functions, procedures, triggers, and other elements.

99: Explain Default Schema for Groups.

Answer:

The default schema for groups is the security feature request from the SQL community implemented in the 2012 version. The default schema for groups can be defined by using the command CREATE USER or ALTER USER (the DEFAULT_SCHEMA options). If no schema options are defined in a group, then SQL Server assumes 'dbo' as the schema by default.

100: Where are audit enhancements?

Answer:

Audit enhancements are found in the following areas:

a) Record filtering
b) User-defined audit event
c) All SKUS
d) Improved resilience
e) T-SQL stack

101: What is an extended event?

Answer:

Extended event is an event handling system for SQL server that supports the correlation of data from SQL Server or from the Operation system or from the database application. It provides a framework for SQL Server audit that results in fast performance and throughput.

102: Write a query that creates a DB and creates schema and tables in that DB.

Answer:

The below queries create a DB, schema, and tables:

```
Create database mydb;
GO
Use mydb;
GO
Create schema myschema;
GO
Create table myschema.generaldata (ID int primary key,
Field1 varchar(100) not null);
```

GO

Create table myschema.sensitivedata (ID int primary key, Field1 varchar(100) not null);

GO

103: What is the benefit of Record Filtering?

Answer:

Record Filtering is used to set up a filter to exclude the application account from being audited when accessing a particular table. For example, when an application accesses the table with an application account there is no need to audit the activity. However when a user accesses the table from outside the application, the event is audited. Use Record Filter to exclude auditing.

104: Write a query that will create the DB audit specification in myNewschema.

Answer:

The following query will create the DB audit specification in myNewschema:

```
Create DB audit specification [SpecifyFilterForSensitiveData]
For Server Audit [SpecifyAuditDataAccess]
ADD (select schema:: [myNewschema]
By [public]) with (STATE = ON);
GO
```

So, when the query is triggered on 'SensitiveData' table, the table will be audited.

105: What are the common features supported for audit and

compliance needs?

Answer:

There are two features supported for audit and compliance needs:

a) Server Audit Specification

b) Database Audit Specification

106: What are the steps to perform to enable contained DB authentication in Management studio?

Answer:

The following steps need to be performed to enable contained DB (database) authentication in SQL Server Management Studio:

a) In Object Explorer, right click the server instance and click properties

b) Select the Advanced page. From 'Containment' section, we have to set "Enable Contained Databases" as True and click OK

107: What are the steps to perform to enable contained DB authentication with Transact-SQL?

Answer:

Use sp_configure option to enable contained DB (database) authentication for a SQL server instance, as in the following queries:

sp_configure SET 'contained DB authentication' AS 1;
GO;

When the option is set to 0, the contained databases are not supported.

108: What are the alternatives for Audit log failure?

Answer:

The alternatives for Audit log failure are as follows:

a) **On Audit:** Shut down Server: If data could not be written to audit log, system will shut down automatically. This is performed to achieve security compliance

b) **Continue:** On Audit log failure: This option allows server to continue operation if data could not be written to audit log. The system will continue to write events to the audit log but records are not retained during failure

c) **Fail Operation:** On Audit log failure: If this option is selected, the server will fail transactions if it can't write events to the audit log. However, transactions not governed by audit will continue to process

109: What are the enhancements to improve resilience other than audit log failures?

Answer:

The additional audit enhancements to improve resilience other than audit log failures include:

a) Max_Files has been introduced when using file as the audit destination. This option caps the amount of audit files to be used without roll over

b) Using the stack frame of Transact-SQL we can determine if a SQL query is issued through an application or from a stored procedure

c) Sp_audit_write procedure allows applications to write customized information to the audit log because the audit specifications support a user-defined audit group

d) Users associated with contained databases can be audited

e) Additional column values were added to sys.fn_get_audit_file, sys.server_audits, and sys.server_file_audits mainly to track the user- defined audit events

110: Write a query to create audit with Fail Operation.

Answer:

The below query creates an audit with Transact-SQL using fail operation:

```
Create server audit [Audit-SQL1]
To file
(FilePath = N'/usr/auditlog',
Maxsize = 5 gb,
Max_files = 50,
Reserve_disk_space = on
)
With
(queue_delay = 500,
On_failure=fail_operation
)
GO
```

111: What is the benefit of a user-defined audit event?

Answer:

A user defined audit event allows the application to create custom events so that the events are registered in the audit log, which allows more flexibility in storing the audit information.

112: How is a user authenticated against a DB without a login that resides in the engine?

Answer:

The user information related to the login credentials is stored in user DB (database) directly, but it is not stored in master database when using the contained databases. This is how the user is authenticated against the DB when the user details reside in the engine.

113: What are the benefits of contained database?

Answer:

The following are the benefits of contained database:

a) The Windows users are authenticated without login

b) Authentication is robust because users can't perform DB instance level operations - only DML operations inside the user DB

c) It eliminates unused logins in the DB instance

114: Use a query to create a contained database user with a password.

Answer:

The following query will create a contained database user with a password:

    Create user tester
    With password='myDBpass$1',
        Default_Language = [English],

Default_schema = [dbo]

GO

115: Use a query to create a contained database user with a domain login.

Answer:

The below query will create a contained database user with a domain login:

Use mydb;

GO

Create user [googlers\testuser];

GO

116: What are the security concerns of contained DB authentication?

Answer:

Though a contained database is a great way to achieve portability, it has the following security concerns:

a) Users can grant and create users without admin privileges
b) If a user gains access, they could access another DB in the engine if the guest account is enabled
c) It is possible to create duplicate logins, which can lead to denial-of service

Chapter 5

Programmability and Beyond-Relational Enhancements

117: What is Beyond Relational in SQL Server?

Answer:

Beyond Relational is the term used collectively for components that have become necessary to be stored in a database other than the conventional Relation Data. When Objects were added to the relational database, it became Object Relational where each database and its tables everything were considered as objects. Now XML, Location data, Office documents, Podcasts, media files, chat scripts, images, mails and various other types of information are available which have to be stored in relation to each record. These new data types are collectively called Beyond-Relational. These are a part of SQL Server 2008 release. XML plays a big role in going Beyond Relational.

118: What are the components of Beyond Relational?

Answer:

All data that need to be stored and that are not of the available basic data types are Beyond Relational. Chat Scripts, Media files, Office documents, Images, Location data, CLR, XML, medical data are all data components that are Beyond Relational. To store these special components, SQL Server 2008 and the later releases contain some special data types such as CLR, XML, hierarchyid, bit, sql_variant, table, sysname, alias and timestamp data types. The XML data type is already revolutionary and has become a part of databases. The CLR data type is considered the next revolutionary inclusion as it can contain triggers, stored procedures, types, aggregate functions and functions. The CLR program can be included as a user-defined type for better encapsulation.

119: Explain the special data types hierarchyid, bit, sql_variant, table, sysname, alias and timestamp data types.

Answer:

The hierarchyid data type is used to store hierarchical tables and data. Hierarchyid functions are used to manage this data. Bit is basically a numeric data type that stores 0 or 1. Sql_variant data type lets the column store different data types for each instance. Each instance of sql_variant data type will store the metadata associated to it. The table data type is like a temporary table. This can be used for creating tables on-the-run. The sysname data type is basically same as a varchar(128) data type. It can contain the name of a table, procedure etc. The alias data type can be used instead of another basic data type and a special procedure can be written to validate it. The timestamp data type is in no way related to a date or time. It is basically a binary number that denotes the order in which the data has been modified in the database. It keeps changing with every update of the row.

120: Can you use a user-defined data type created in one database in another database?

Answer:

Typically, a user-defined data type defined in one database is local to that database and cannot be accessed in another database. But if you want to access the same user-defined type in more than one database, you have to define the same in the same way in both the databases and then it can be used across both databases. Another option is to use the tempdb database. Since a temporary table only is created, the data types need not be defined in it. So you can load the data in the table of one database into a temporary table and then access it within the program or procedure. But when you are creating user-defined data type to be used across 2 databases, make sure that their names and basic data types match. Also make sure you have permission for EXECUTE and SELECT on the data type in both databases.

121: What does beyond-relational enhancement mean?

Answer:

Beyond-relational enhancement refers to the following features:

a) **Full-text search:** Character-based data search in SQL Server tables

b) **Spatial data:** Objects like images, videos, etc

c) **File stream:** Unstructured data in SQL Server

122: What are the new beyond-relational enhancements features introduced in SQL Server 2012?

Answer:

The following are the new beyond-relational enhancements features introduced in SQL Server 2012:

a) **File Tables:** A special table that stores files that can be accessed from Windows applications as if they were stored in a file system

b) **Statistical Semantic Searches:** This search queries the word and its respective meaning from SQL Server tables

123: Explain File Stream.

Answer:

File Stream in SQL Server allows the storing of unstructured data in the database. Files with images, videos, and other such files stored in the file system are referred as unstructured data and are stored in SQL Server tables using File Stream.

124: What are the new File Stream enhancements in SQL Server 2012?

Answer:

The following are the File Stream features introduced in SQL Server 2012:

a) Support for file groups and Multiple Storage containers to attain maximum-scale up functionality

b) Support for adding additional storage drives to improve the scaling flexibility

125: Explain beyond-relational features by using an example.

Answer:

Beyond-relational can be explained with the following example: An e-mail inbox application like 'Microsoft Outlook' stores both structured and unstructured data. The application comes with a search text through which we can search full-text search and retrieve both structured and unstructured data. Further, the application also provides semantic search that finds related messages stored in the application.

126: Explain RBS.

Answer:

RBS refers to Remote Blob Store. This feature was introduced in SQL Server 2008 to handle unstructured data. With the RBS API (Application Programming Interface), we can store a BLOB (Binary Large Object) such as an image, video etc. in a vendor independent API. This API has BLOB IDs stored inside the database to manage consistency. With the BLOB ID, we can query the specific BLOB data that exists in the remote machine.

127: What are the limitations of RBS?

Answer:

There are three limitations to using RBS:

a) It does not provide support for full-text search (Character based search)

b) It does not provide support for transactional integration between two servers

c) Database administrators can tie relational data with RBS data in a loosely coupled manner (read-only support)

128: What is a FileTable?
Answer:
FileTable refers to a new user table which gets created in the Database Engine. It has a fixed schema that contains file attributes and FILESTREAM. So, FileTable makes use of the FILESTREAM feature that stores images, documents, video, etc. in the SQL Server table. So, whenever images, documents, videos, etc. are stored in a FileTable, it can be accessed as if we were accessing the Windows file system.

129: What are the prerequisites for FileTable?
Answer:
There are three prerequisites for FileTable:

a) The FILESTREAM has to be enabled at SQL Server's DB (Database) Engine instance level

b) Non-transactional Access has to be enabled at the SQL Server Database level

c) Ensure a directory is specified to store files at the SQL Server Database level

130: What are the steps to be performed to enable

FILESTREAM?

Answer:

These steps must be performed to enable FILESTREAM using SQL Server configuration manager:

a) Select SQL Server Configuration Manager from 'All Programs --> Microsoft SQL Server 2012' start menu

b) Highlight SQL Server services in the left pane

c) Then, Select SQL Server instance from which you want to enable FILESTRAM and click the 'properties'

d) Enable FILESTREAM for Transact-SQL access, on the FILESTREAM tab

e) Then, enable FILESTREAM for Input Output File Access so that we can read and write data

f) Then, select 'Provide Remote Client Access to FILESTREAM data'

g) Then click apply and choose OK to close the SQL properties

131: How are enable directory and non-transactional access for FileTable accomplished?

Answer:

The following steps have to be performed in SQL Server Management studio to enable directory and non-transactional access:

a) Select the SQL Server DB instance to create a FileTable

b) Right-click the database and select the 'Properties' option

c) Select 'Option' page from the properties dialog window

d) In the FILESTREAM Directory name Text box, insert the

name of the directory

e) In the Non-Transacted Access option, select either Full or Read-Only option

f) Then select Ok to close the dialog box

132: What are the steps to enable directory and Non-transactional access using Transact-SQL?

Answer:

Enable directory and Non-transactional access using Transact-SQL with the following query:

```
USE [master]

GO

Alter Database [MyDataBase] set FILESTREAM
(NON_TRANSACTED_ACCESS = READ-ONLY,
DIRECTORY_NAME = N'MyDir') with NO_WAIT

GO
```

In the above query, we have created a directory called 'MyDir' and provided read-only option for Non-transactional access.

133: How is File Stream file groups using Transact-SQL configured?

Answer:

Configure File Stream file groups using Transact-SQL with the following query:

```
USE [master]

GO

Alter Database [MyDataBase]
ADD FILEGROUP [MyFileGroup] contains FILESTREAM
```

GO

In the above query, a file group called 'MyFileGroup' was created in the database 'MyDB'.

134: How are database files created using Transact-SQL?

Answer:

Create database files using Transact-SQL with the following query:

USE [master]

GO

Alter Database [MyDataBase]

ADD FILE (NAME = N'MyStreamFile',
FILENAME=N'D:\Test\MyStreamFile')

TO FILEGROUP [MyFileGroup]

GO

In the above query, a file called 'MyStreamFile' was created in the location 'D:\Test' and added the file to the file group called 'MyFileGroup' in the database 'MyDB'.

135: How is a FileTable created using Transact-SQL?

Answer:

Create a FileTable using Transact-SQL with the following query:

USE MYDataBase

GO

Create table MyDataBaseTable as FILETABLE

GO

In the above query, a FileTable called 'MyTable' was created.

136: What are the steps needed in Management Studio to create FileTable?

Answer:

The following steps have to be performed in SQL Server Management Studio to create FileTable:

a) Select the database in object explorer where the FileTable is to be created

b) Select a table, right-click, and choose 'New FileTable' option

c) This opens a SQL window in which to write the query (create table MyNewTable as FILETABLE) and execute the query

This will create a FileTable calle MYNewTable on the selected table.

137: What are the performance and scalability improvements achieved using full text search?

Answer:

The full text search in SQL Server 2012 can now scale (ability to search) from 100 million documents to 350 million documents. This query performance is 7 to 10 times faster when compared with the previous version.

138: What are the new functionalities of full text search?

Answer:

Full text search provides three new functionalities:

a) **Property search:** The option to search file properties (Example: titles that exist in a document)

b) **Word breaks:** This breaks the word from the content using semantic search feature

c) **Custom Proximity Operator:** This is also referred to as 'customizable near' and it is used to identify how close the search term appears to another term in a particular document

139: Explain custom proximity operator with an example.

Answer:

Custom proximity operator is used to find a particular word if that exists near another word. For example to find the word 'query' that exists before the word 'insert' in a particular document we use the custom proximity operator.

For example; Select * from MyTable where contains (*, 'near((query, insert), 6, false)')

In the above query we are using near to identify if the word query exists exactly 6 tokens before insert.

140: Explain statistical semantic search.

Answer:

The statistical semantic search is a new feature in SQL Server 2012 which extends full text search and provides the exact meaning of the actual phrase. This search also identifies the meaning of the particular search phrase and provides the exact match for the particular phrase from the unstructured documents that exists in the database engine.

141: How will you identify if semantic search is configured for a

database?

Answer:

Identify whether semantic search is configured using the below query:

Select serverproperty('IsFullTextInstalled')

GO

If the value is returned as 1, then semantic search is configured. If the value is returned as 0, then semantic search is not configured.

142: Explain spatial data.

Answer:

Spatial data refers to geographic location and boundaries of data that are related to earth but not limited to oceans, land, natural features, constructed features, etc. This spatial data is stored as coordinates as a vector data format that can be mapped internally to the tables.

143: What are the types of spatial data?

Answer:

There are two types of spatial data:

a) **Geometry data type:** This data type refers to flat earth data such as image analysis and shape analysis

b) **Geographic data type:** This refers to the round earth data such as GPS coordinates of latitude and longitude

144: What are the spatial data features that are supported in SQL Server?

Answer:

The following spatial data features are supported in SQL Server 2012:

a) **Point:** A zero dimensional object that represents an elevation and a measuring value

b) **Multipoint:** A collection of zero or more point

c) **LineString:** A one dimensional object which connects two points

d) **MultiLineString:** A collection of zero or more line strings

e) **Polygon** - A two dimensional object that connects multiple points and form a shape

f) **MultiPolygon:** A collection of zero or more polygons

g) **Collection:** A collection of zero or more geometry or graphical instances

145: Explain Extended Event using an example.

Answer:

Extended Event is an event handling system in SQL Server which supports correlation of data from the database application and operating system. The following are the extended systems that are introduced in SQL Server 2012:

a) **page_allocated:** This event contains the following fields: page_location, page_size, number_pages, worker_address, pool_id, allocator_type, and page_allocator_type

b) **page_freed:** This event also contains the same fields as that of page_allocated

c) **allocation_failure:** This event contains the following fields: failure_type, allocation_failure_type, worker_address, factor, and pool_id

This page is intentionally left blank.

Chapter 6

Integration Services

146: Explain SQL Server Integration Services. How is it different from DTS?

Answer:

SQL Server integration Services or SSIS is the next version of DTS or Data Transmission Services. The SSIS works in an enterprise level and is extensively used in data warehousing to Extract, Transform and Load (ETL) data data in a fast and flexible way. Extraction, migration and consolidation of data from different relational databases is made possible easily using SSIS. It also takes data from sources like XML data files and normal data files, processes it and loads the processed data into an enterprise level data warehouse or other systems. The SQL Server Data Tools is an integral part of SSIS which helps in development and testing these integration programs. It also contains, a server component where these programs can be deployed and run.

147: Explain a Container and the type of containers available in SQL Server.

Answer:

A container in SSIS is a coherent collection of tasks which lets you administer the scale of the tasks collectively. There are basically 3 types of containers available in the IDE and a fourth one which is the container of all containers. The Sequence container is used to group rationally related tasks together. The For Loop container is used when the same set of tasks have to be repeated. The For Each Loop container is used to traverse through each object in the collection like a record set or a file list. The container of all containers is called the Task Host Container.

148: Explain an SSIS breakpoint and how to configure, disable and delete it!

Answer:

Data Transmission involves breaking of large volume of data into small packages and sending these small packages through the network. Each package will contain the information regarding what it contains and how it will related to the other set of packages. In SSIS, a breakpoint is applied to specific objects which can be later used to review the data sent and received to confirm there's not loss of data during transmission. The SQL Server Business Intelligence Studio or BIDS has the option in its control flow interface to select an object and set the breakpoint to it on upto 10 different conditions. Single or multiple conditions can be selected for each breakpoint. This makes authenticating the data easily. To disable and delete the SSIS breakpoint also you have to go through BIDS option.

149: Explain Precedence Constraint. Explain the types of Precedence Constraint in SQL Server.

Answer:

You can place many tasks in the SSIS control flow and connect them using Precedence Constraint connectors. It is basically a used to define the order in which these tasks are to be executed and the conditions based on which they need to be executed. The Precedence Constraints can be Success, Failure or Complete. Success Precedence Constraint means the next task can be taken up only when the last task is successfully completed. Failure Precedence Constraint will imply that the next task will be executed only if the last task fails. Complete Precedence Constraint means, the next task can be executed irrespective of whether the last task was a Success or a Failure.

150: Explain SQL Server Integration Services.

Answer:

Integration Services is a service platform for building data integration and data transformation solutions at the enterprise level. It is mainly used for solving business problems like sending messages, updating data warehouses, downloading files, cleaning data, and to manage SQL objects and data. It can also transform data from other sources like flat files, XML files, relational data sources, and load data to more than one destination.

151: What templates are available for using Integration Services?

Answer:

There are two templates available for Integration Services:

a) **Integration Services Project Template:** This template is used to add tasks and order those tasks into workflows

b) **Integration Service Import Project Wizard:** This wizard is used to import a project from a project deployment file or use this option as a starting point for a new project

152: What are the new features available in Integration Services Interface?

Answer:

The new features available in the Integration Services interface are:

a) **Getting Started:** A video describing how to use and work with Integration Services

b) **SSIS Toolbox:** SQL Server Integration Services Toolbox provides options to add tasks and data flow components

c) **Zoom control:** This changes the normal view to a maximum of 500% and to a minimum of 10%

d) **Variables button:** This button on the designer toolbar provides access to declare variables

e) **Parameters:** This option species run time values to the variables

f) **SSIS Toolbox button:** This button on the designer toolbar opens SSIS Toolbox when it is not visible from the Integration Services Interface

153: Explain Scripting Engine.

Answer:

Scripting Engine in SQL Server Integration Services is an upgrade to VSTA 3.0 (Visual Studio Tools for Applications) and includes support for .NET Framework 4.0. When editing a script task in the control or data flow, the VSTA IDE (Integrated Development Environment) opens in a separate window and enables the VSTA debug features. This is a significant improvement to the scripting engine.

154: How are Expression Indicators used in Integration Services?

Answer:

The expressions in Integration Services are used to create a flexible package. They are used with a connection manager to dynamically change connection strings to accommodate movement of package from one environment to another (Example: Development to Production). Also, if you add an expression to a variable or task, the indicator will appear on that object.

155: Explain the new Undo and Redo feature in SSDT.

Answer:

Undo and Redo is a new feature available while developing packages in SQL Server Data Tools. In SSDT, We can make edits either in control flow or in data flow and use undo to reverse a change and redo to restore the change. This feature also works in the Variables window and in the Event Handlers and Parameter tabs of Integration Services.

156: Explain SQL Server Integration Services Control Flow.

Answer:

Control Flow in SQL Server is defined as the workflow of tasks to be executed in a sequential fashion. By definition:

a) Control flow, specifies the sequence of the process (which contains tasks) to be performed

b) The smallest unit in control flow is a task

c) The first task has to be completed before beginning task 2

d) It does not have control on data in each task

For example, in the case of opening a bank account, first fill out the form, then data is verified by the banker, and then a background check is performed by the banker for data correctness, and finally an account is created. Representing this sequence of steps in a diagram is referred to as the control flow in SQL Server.

157: Explain SQL Server Integration Services Data Flow.

Answer:

Data Flow in SQL Server Integration Services refers to streaming data being passed between components. Data Flow is often defined as the flow of data from a source to a destination and Data flows between sources, transformation and destination.

For example, assume the need to extract data from an XML file, then sort the data and write it in a flat file. Here the XML file is the source, sorting the data is transformation and the destination is a flat file.

158: What are the default control flow tasks in SSIS?

Answer:

The following are the commonly available control flow tasks in SQL Server Integration Services:

a) **For Each Loop container:** This allows to loop through files, collections, XML nodes and various objects

b) **Execute SQL Task:** This task could execute a stored procedure or an SQL query

c) **FTP Task:** This sends or receives files through File Transfer Protocol

d) **Execute Package Task:** This allows a child package within current package context

e) **Send Mail Task:** This sends an email through SMTP

f) **Script Task:** This uses a VB.NET script to perform advanced scripting

159: What are the new tasks added to Control Flow in SSIS?
Answer:

The new tasks are added to Control Flow in SQL Server Integration Services:

a) **Expression Task:** Evaluates the expression during package workflow

b) **Execute Package Task:** Configures the relationship between the parent package and the child package

c) **Change Data Capture Task:** Creates a capture instance in order to track each table

160: Explain Expression Task in SSIS.
Answer:

Expression Task is the new feature available in SSIS (SQL Server
Integration Services) toolbox when the control flow tab is selected.
The main purpose of Expression Task is to easily assign a dynamic
value to the variable. Instead of using Script Task to construct
variable value at run time, now add Expression Task to the
workflow and use SSIS Expression Language.

161: Explain Execute Package Task.

Answer:

Execute Package Task is a feature in Integration Services that
allows the packages to execute other packages as part of workflow
execution.

For example: assume there are 2 tasks - Script Task and Send Mail
task. To execute a Script task (Example: Update DB record)
whenever a mail is sent, configure the Execute Package Task in
Send Mail task.

162: What are the new features introduced in Execute Package Task in SSIS 2012?

Answer:

In Execute Package Task, a new property 'ReferenceType' has
been included. This new property appears in the Execute
Package's Task editor. The new property 'ReferenceType' is used
to mention the package location to be executed.

For example: if the Script task exists in a file system location, then
we can configure the Script task location in the ReferenceType
property.

Also, the Execute Package Task editor has a new interface to configure parameter bindings i.e., using this interface; we can map a parameter from the child package to parameter value in the parent package.

163: What is deployment model?

Answer:

Deployment model is a deployment technique for deploying SQL Server Integration Service projects and packages that are created using SSDT (SQL Server Data Tools). The deployment is performed through the Integration Services interface.

164: What are the deployment models supported in SSIS?

Answer:

There are two deployment models supported in SQL Server Integration Services:

a) **Package deployment model:** A package can be deployed to a file system or to a database in a SQL Server DB instance

b) **Project deployment model:** Used to deploy the projects that are created in SQL Server Data Tools to the SQL Server Integration Services

165: What is Project Deployment Workflow?

Answer:

Project Deployment Workflow is the process of converting design time objects in SQL Server Data Tools to database objects in SQL Server Integration Services. It is also the process of retrieving database objects from the integration service in order to update a package or use an existing package as a template for a new package.

166: What are the stages of Project Deployment workflow?

Answer:

The four stages of Project Deployment workflow are:

a) **Build:** In this stage the packages are compressed as a single unit

b) **Deploy:** In this stage the packages are deployed to SQL Server Integration Service

c) **Import:** In this stage the package can be imported from SQL Server catalog

d) **Convert:** In this stage the packages and configuration files are converted to the latest version of Integration services

167: What properties are used to configure project parameters?

Answer:

The following are properties used to add project parameters:

a) **Description:** An optional property used to specify the instruction for an administrator for managing packages that are deployed to the project catalog

b) **Sensitive:** The value of this property is False by default. If this is set to True, the parameter values are encrypted when you deploy the project to the catalog

c) **Required:** The value of this property is False by default. If this is set to True, then we must configure the parameter value for the parameter we create for the package

168: What are execution parameter values?

Answer:

The execution parameter values can be applied only to a specific execution of a package.

Set the execution parameter value by using the catalog.set_execution_parameter_value stored procedure as shown below. The value can't be set using SQL Server Management Studio.

```
set_execution_parameter_value [
    @execution_id = execution_id, [ @object_type = ]
    object_type
    , [ @parameter_name = ] parameter_name
    , [ @parameter_value = ] parameter_value
```

The stored procedure above sets the execution parameter values for a particular package.

169: What is Integration Services Catalog?

Answer:

Integration Services Catalog is a new feature that is used to support the administration of packages, centralization of storage, and related configuration information. Each SQL Server instance can host only one catalog. If the project is deployed using project deployment model, the component and the project is added to the Integration Services catalog and administrators can manage the project.

170: What is the use of encryption in SSIS?

Answer:

Encryption is used in SQL Server Integration Services to protect sensitive parameter values. If anyone tries to retrieve sensitive parameter values using SQL Server Management Studio or Transact-SQL, the parameter value will be displayed as a NULL value protecting the data.

171: What are the various encryptions supported in SSIS?
Answer:
The following encryption algorithms are supported in SQL Server Integration Services:
   a) **AES_256:** This algorithm is supported by default. AES refers to Advanced Encryption Standard. It supports 256 bit keys
   b) **AES_192:** This supports 192 bit keys
   c) **AES_128:** This supports 128 bit keys
   d) **DES:** This refers to Data Encryption Standard. This is considered as insecure when compared to AES
   e) **TRIPLE_DES:** This refers to Triple Data Encryption Standard. This handles 64 bit keys
   f) **DESX:** This is created to increase the complexity of hacking using key whitening technique

172: What is environment reference? What are its types?
Answer:
Environment reference is a project property used to connect the environment variables (SQL Server instance specific) to a parameter. There are two types if environment reference:
   a) **Relative Environment Reference:** In this case, the parent folder of environment folder must be the parent folder for

project folder

b) **Absolute Environment Reference:** In this case, the folder for environment and project can exist in any location

173: What are the monitoring or troubleshooting tools available in SSIS?

Answer:

There are three types of monitoring or troubleshooting tools available in SQL Server Integration Services:

a) **Package Execution Logs:** This captures information related to project environment, memory, page size, and available CPUs

b) **Reports:** This provides the package execution results of last 24 hours

c) **Data Taps:** This is a Data Viewer used to capture data during package execution. The captured data is stored in a CSV file that could be viewed once the execution is completed

174: Describe the security of Integration Services.

Answer:

In Integration Services, the packages and related objects are stored securely in the catalog using encryption algorithm. Only members of SQL Server database have access to all objects in the catalog and perform operations like create catalog, create folders in catalog, execute stored procedures, etc. To provide folder level access, Administrators use MANAGE_OBJECT_PERMISSIONS to grant access to a particular user. We can also set the grant or deny permissions for each user to secure projects, operations, environments, and folders.

Chapter 7

Data Quality Services

175: What are SQL Server's Data Quality Service? Explain briefly the different DQS processes.

Answer:

DQS or Data Quality Services is an SQL Server tool which makes sure the quality of data maintained and retrieved are good. It allows the user to create a knowledge base and based on that ensures that the data is consistent, complete and accurate. DQS either performs or lets us to perform monitoring, profiling, cleansing and matching of data. The tracking facility helps us to track the progress of DQS as well as the quality of data. It also keeps track of the source of the data and verifies it at different stages. The source of data can give some information regarding its quality which is required in the various stages of DQS. The cleansing process involves verifying against external references also such as Windows Azure Marketplace, to correct, standardize and enrich the data. DQS marks the data are correct, corrected, not corrected, auto corrected or new. The user can accept or reject the data marked as auto-corrected or new data. Matching refers to removing duplicate entries. DQS identifies, links and merges related data whenever found.

176: How can DQS help in a Business?
Answer:
All businesses depend on data which has to be accurate. Data accuracy is a key factor to customer satisfaction and the progress of the business. Inconsistent data or incorrect data can jeopardise the business in many ways. While consolidating the data for business reports, inconsistent data will result in irrational results and it will affect the decision-making process. DQS provides a simple solution to maintain data quality with proper references and processing. One simple example is the date validation done on external data sources. If an employee's birthdate is wrongly entered as 29/Feb/2011 in the excel file which has no validation, DQS alerts it to the user to correct the same.

177: What are Reference Data Services in DQS?
Answer:
Reference Data Services or RDS refers to the external sources that can be used as a reference for DQS cleansing and correction. The external resources can be a Microsoft Azure Marketplace or some other third party reference data vendors. This ensures a wider reference for DQS other than the organization's internal knowledge base. Once these references are bought or subscribed

to, they can be configured and then added to the DQS reference table. this is a one-time job for the DBS administrator. This can be later used for cleansing the data by setting the proper parameters to use the desired external references also during the process.

178: What happens during DQS profiling and notification?
Answer:
DQS Profiling checks the data source for any errors and alerts the user with the possible corrections suggested. The user can either choose one of the suggested corrections or input a new correction. Corrections input by the user are also analysed and accepted only when they are found correct. DQS Profiling gives the user an idea about the data source's quality. It checks the entire data source and provides the user with a review of the data based on its quality. Profiling alerts always require remedial actions which are either suggested or has to be provided by the user. It checks the source against the knowledge base. The existing data is checked against the data source and based on the history, notifications are given to make sure the desired data accuracy is achieved.

179: Explain the function Data Quality Services.
Answer:
DQS (Data Quality Services) provides a solution for database administrators to maintain quality of data and ensure data is suited for business usage.

It also provides an interactive, knowledge-driven solution to manage the quality and integrity of the data sources.

DQS also enables administrators to discover, build, and manage data and perform profiling, matching, and data cleansing.

180: What features of DQS are used to resolve data quality issue?

Answer:

These are the features of Data Quality Services used to resolve data quality issues:

a) **Monitoring:** This tracks the data quality activities and enables us to verify that the data quality solution does for it was designed to do

b) **Matching:** This identifies the duplicates and enables us to determine what constitutes a match and perform re-duplication

c) **Data Cleansing:** This removes, modifies, and enrich the data that is incorrect or incomplete

d) **Knowledge base:** This enables us to analyze data and create quality process to enhance the knowledge of our data and thereby continuously improve the quality of data

e) **Profiling:** This is a powerful tool in DQS through which we can create a data quality solution

181: What are the components of DQS?

Answer:

There are two components in Data Quality Services used to perform quality services that are independent from other SQL operations. These two components are:

a) **Data Quality Server:** This manages the storage of knowledge and executes knowledge related processes

b)   **Data Quality Client:** This is a standalone application used
     to perform administration activities and knowledge
     management in one interface

**182: What databases are installed during installation of Data
Quality Server?**

Answer:

The Data Quality Server will install the following databases:

a)   **DQS_MAIN:** The primary database containing the
     published knowledge and stored procedures that support
     DQS engine

b)   **DQS_PROJECTS:** For internal use to store data related to
     data quality projects and managing knowledge bases

c)   **DQS_STAGING_DATA:** Used for intermediate data
     storage to perform DQS operations and to store processed
     data

**183: What roles must be mapped for each user before using
DQS_MAIN database?**

Answer:

The following roles must be mapped to each user during
installation of DQS_MAIN database before using the service:

a)   **dqs_kb_editor:** This role is used to create and edit the
     knowledge base

b)   **dqs_kb_operator:** This role is used to edit and execute
     data quality projects and to monitor data

c)   **dqs_administrator:** This role can perform the operations
     of an editor and operator; they can add new users, stop

any activity, stop a process within an activity, and perform any configuration using Data Quality client

184: What are the tasks available in Data Quality Client?

Answer:

There are three types of tasks available in Data Quality Client:

a) **Administration:** View the status of data quality projects and knowledge base management that are used in Integration Services

b) **Knowledge Base Management:** Create a new knowledge base or edit the existing knowledgebase

c) **Data Quality projects:** Create and execute data quality projects to perform data-cleansing and data matching tasks

185: Explain Knowledge Base Management.

Answer:

Knowledge base management in Data Quality Service refers to storing information including valid and invalid values, and thereby applying rules for validating and correcting data. A knowledge base is created from sample data or creates a new one from scratch.

186: What activities are performed using Knowledge base?

Answer:

Following activities can be performed using knowledge base in Data Quality Client:

a) **Domain Management:** This is used to manage the

knowledge base contents and its rules. Only one user at a time can perform the domain management activity for a single knowledge base

b) **Matching Policy:** This contains one or more matching rules to determine the probability of matching between two records. This is also used to correct data problems like misspelled client names or inconsistent address formats

c) **Knowledge Discovery:** This is used to partially automate the process of adding knowledge to the database. We perform this activity to add domain values to the knowledge base from one or more data sources

187: When you create a new domain for a knowledge base, what are the properties that need to be configured?

Answer:

These properties need to be configured when creating a new domain for a knowledge base:

a) **Domain Name:** A unique domain name within knowledge base; it supports a maximum of 256 characters

b) **Data Type:** The data types that can be configured are Integer, Decimal, Date and String

c) **Description:** An optional property used to specify more information about the contents of domain; a maximum of 2048 characters are supported

d) **Normalize String:** This appears only when selecting the data type as String. It removes special characters (like punctuation marks) and improves the accuracy of matches when we re-duplicate data

e) **Language:** Applicable only for String data type; a language is selected in order to check for spelling of content

f) **Disable syntax error algorithm:** Before adding values to the domain, Data Quality Service will check for Syntax errors of string values; the option is to enable or disable syntax error checking

g) **Enable speller:** This option will check the spelling of domain values

h) **Format Output:** Format the domain values according to the data type chosen. For example, if the data type is Date, then the format can be specified as DD-MM-YYYY

188: What are the types of settings to configure for domain value?

Answer:

Configure three types of settings for domain values. They are:

a) **Correct:** If the domain values have no syntax errors, then specify the setting as correct

b) **Invalid:** If the domain value is not a member of the domain, then specify the setting as Invalid. For example: the value of 'United Kingdom' is an invalid value in a Product domain

c) **Error:** If the domain value is misspelled or it contains improper abbreviation, then specify the setting as Error. For example, 'I/P is text O/P is String' has to be specified as Error and include the correct abbreviation as 'Input is text and Output is String'

189: Explain RDS.

Answer:

RDS (Reference Data Services) refers to an accurate and complete set of related and categorized global data available at trusted public domains and from commercial content providers. RDS enables us to enrich our business data and validate the data by subscribing to third party data providers. This reference data process is incorporated in the knowledge base data quality project to achieve comprehensive quality of data.

190: How is reference data used to cleanse data?

Answer:

Cleansing data in Data Quality Service by using the reference data involves the following three steps:

a) **Configure reference data in DQS:** If using an online data provider, add the data provider details in Data Quality Service before using

b) **Map domain in knowledge base to the reference data:** Specify the domain name to the reference data service that is added or subscribed

c) **Use mapped domains in data quality project for cleansing:** To clean the activity, we have to select the knowledge base that contains domains names which are mapped with the reference data services

191: What is the need for a matching policy?

Answer:

Matching policy is needed for data quality projects to correct data problems such as inconsistent address formats or misspelled customer names. It is also needed to determine the probability of a match between two records by applying one or more matching rules. It is also needed to add knowledge to the knowledge base based on the data that exists in the data quality services.

192: What are the steps involved when creating a cleansing data quality project?
Answer:
There are four steps involved in creating a cleaning data quality project:

a) **Map:** The first step is to map the data source to the domains in the selected knowledge base. The source can be an Excel file, view, or table in SQL Server database

b) **Cleanse:** Data Quality service uses advanced algorithms to cleanse data and calculate a confidence score to determine the category applicable to each record in the source data

c) **Manage and View Results:** In this step, review separate tabs (New, Suggested, Correct, Corrected and Invalid) for each group of records characterized by Data Quality Service

d) **Export:** In this step, export the results of cleansing data quality project to a CSV file or a SQL Server table

193: Explain Matching Projects.
Answer:
With the help of a Matching Policy defined for a knowledge base, a matching data quality project can identify both approximate and

exact matches in a data source. We can execute the matching process after executing the cleansing process and exporting the results. We can then specify the destination table or export file as the source for the matching project

194: What are the steps involved in a matching data quality project?

Answer:

There are three steps involved in matching data quality project. They are:

a) **Map:** The first step in matching project is the cleansing project to map the fields from the source to a domain

b) **Matching:** In this step, choose whether to generate overlapping or non-overlapping clusters and launch the automated matching process

c) **Export:** After matching results are reviewed, export the result as the final step of the matching project

195: What are the export options available for exporting contents in matching data quality project?

Answer:

There are two export options available to export the contents in matching data quality project:

a) **Matching Results:** This content type includes both matched and unmatched records. This includes the matched or unmatched records, the matching rule applied to identify the match, matching score, and the approval status

b) **Survivorship Results:** This content type includes the survivor ship records and unmatched records

196: What are the steps an Administrator can perform using the features of Data Quality Client?

Answer:

In the Data Quality Client, an administrator can perform the two tasks below:

a) **Activity Monitoring:** Any user provided rights to open Data Quality Client can perform this step

b) **Configuration Task:** This step is performed only by the administrator where the log files and properties are configured

197: What details can be monitored in the Data Quality Client?

Answer:

In the Data Quality Client the monitoring page is used to review the status of current activities and historic activities that are performed on the Data Quality Server. The data quality service administrators can terminate an activity or a step within an activity by right clicking on the activity or step. They can also monitor who initiated the activity, the start time of the activity, the end time of the activity and the elapsed time. They can find the activities by type, subtype, status, or by user.

198: What are the pages that can be exported from Data Quality Client monitoring?

Answer:

The following pages can be exported from the Data Quality Client monitoring page:

a) **Activity:** Includes the details about the activity name, type, sub type, status, and elapsed time

b) **Processes:** Contains details about each activity step which includes current status, start time, end time, and elapsed time

c) **Profiler Source:** The contents of this page depend on the activity sub type. For example, for cleansing subtype it contains: total records, correct records, and invalid records

d) **Profiler Fields:** The contents of this page also depend on the activity sub type. For example, cleansing subtype contains the fields like domain name, corrected value, suggested value, completeness, and accuracy

199: Explain Data Quality Client configuration.

Answer:

The Data Quality client configuration allows three activities. They are:

a) Set up the reference data providers

b) Set properties for the data quality server and

c) Configure logging

To configure logging requires administrator rights and the other two steps do not require administrator rights.

200: Explain Interactive Cleansing and Profiler setting in Data Quality Client configuration.

Answer:

Interactive Cleansing: In this setting, specify the minimum confidence score for suggestions and auto corrections. The Data Quality Services uses these values as thresholds when determining how to categorize records for a cleansing data quality project.

Profiler: In this setting, enable or disable the profiling notifications. The notifications appear in the Profiler tab when we perform a knowledgebase activity or execute a data quality project.

201: Where can one subscribe to reference data?

Answer:

Subscribe to reference data services through the Windows Azure market place. Reference data services are available as a free trial or as a monthly paid subscription. Digital Trowel provides a free service to cleanse and standardize data for public and private companies that are located in United States. When subscribing to a reference data service, an account key is received that must be registered in Data Quality Client before we use reference data in data quality activities.

202: Explain DQS in Integration Services.

Answer:

In Integration Services, use the Data Quality Services components to periodically perform data cleansing in a scheduled time slot; records are categorized as correct, suggested, corrected, and invalid. The Data Quality Services connection manager is used to establish a connection from the Integration Services package to the data quality server. The connection manager has a button to test the connection to the data quality server.

203: Explain DQS in Master Data services.

Answer:

In Master Data Services, compare the external data to the master data in order to find the matching records based on the matching policy we define for the knowledge base. Use the Data Quality Services data matching functionality to re-duplicate master data by creating a matching policy for a Data Quality Service knowledge base.

This page is intentionally left blank.

Chapter 8

Master Data Services

204: What is SQL Master Data Services? Why is it required?

Answer:

Master Data Services or MDS in SQL defines the non-transactional or the master data which is used by the transactions in a business application. This is a platform where the organization defines the business rules, hierarchies, user and role authorities, data versioning and transactions. It includes a MDS Configuration Manager, Master Data manager or the administrator, MDSModelDeploy.exe which is a tool used to deploy the model objects, MDS Web Service and the MDS Excel Add-in. SQL Master Data Services basically includes the components and tools to create and manage model objects that contain the data. It helps to improve the data quality by applying business rules, validations, versions, notifications and security details that are created and managed by the MDS to be applied on master and transaction data entered by the user or taken from other data sources such as a Microsoft Excel data sheet. MDS supports import and export of data and also to create customised applications for maintaining the Master Data.

205: Explain the steps involved in creating and deploying an MDS.

Answer:

Creating an MDS model involves the following steps -

a) First create a model which in simple terms can be the basic categories or group that you deal in.

b) Then create the entities in each model. An entity can be considered as a table which will actually contain the actual members, for example, a Product. The domain-based attributes such as colours or sizes need to be created first which will be used as the values for the entity member.

c) Next we need to define the attributes for the entities such as the weight, cost etc. Every entity will by default have the Name and Code attribute which cannot be changed. If your entity has more attribute, group the related attributes together and create an attribute group. Input or import the base attribute values or the supporting entities such as the colour and sizes.

d) Next step is to create the business rules which can be setting the default value of certain attributes or sending a mail or notification if a particular data does not pass the validation.

e) Now we can input or import data for the basic entities and apply the business rules we just defined. Any corrections in business rules can be done at this stage.

f) The next step is to create derived hierarchies such that any change in the base will automatically reflect in the related entities. Depending on the requirement explicit hierarchies and collections can be defined.

g) Now it is important to create the user-defined metadata. Metadata can be the information regarding the ownership of the object or the source of the data etc.

h) Once the basic members are loaded and passed the business rules set, lock the data with a version tag.

i) You can now create subscription views to view the master data.

j) The last and an important step is to configure the user and group permissions for security reasons. Once these are done successfully, you can deploy your MDS model.

206: Explain how to deploy an MDS model.

Answer:

An MDS model package is usually an XML file that contains the definition of the model and sometimes the data also to be deployed. These are version specific so make sure the versions of SQL in which they were created and are to be deployed are the same. The MDSModelDeploy.exe tool is used to deploy the model package. The Model Deployment Wizard can be used to deploy the model structure but it will not bring in any data. The Model Package Editor can be used to make changes in the deployed model. By default, these tools will be available in the Configuration folder of SQL server MDS.

207: How do you make sure the master data is secure?

Answer:

The Security settings in the MDS model helps us to set and control the user-level and role-level access to the entities in the model. In the User and Group Permissions section, we can create Administrators and User and assign specific entity-level permissions. User permissions can be set for specific functionalities, attributes and the type of access (Read or Edit) to the attributes, or the members and the types of access to the members (Read or Edit). Another important aspect of MDS security is that these security features can be applied to the MS Excel Add-in also. The only difference is that it takes a set period of time, which is usually 20 minutes, for the permission settings to take effect in the Excel. This time interval can be configured in the web.config file.

208: What are the core features of the Master Data Services in SQL Server?

Answer:

Master Data Services (MDS) ensures information integrity and data consistency across the organization. Some of the key features of the MDM include:

a) Master data hub as a data source

b) Automated & Simplified Workflow and Rules definition

c) Support Hierarchies and attributes

209: What are the new improvements of Master Data Services in SQL Server 2012?

Answer:

SQL Server 2012 Master Data Services comes with the following new improvements:

a) Master Data Service is a built-in feature in SQL Server 2012 rather than a separate component

b) Add-in for Excel is a new feature of MDS for managing the master data

c) SharePoint integration

d) Easy data loading with high performance

210: How is MDS installed or upgraded in SQL Server 2012?

Answer:

Master Data Services can be installed or upgraded using Master Data Services Configuration Manager. This tool performs the following options:

a) Create or Upgrade MDS database

b) Configure MDS System settings

c) Create a web application for MDS

New Installation of MDS requires specifying a Microsoft Windows account as MDS administrator and requires IIS server to be installed.

211: Explain the Master Data Manager in MDS.

Answer:

Master Data Manager is a web based application for managing the master data. MDS administrators can manage the object model and configure security settings using this web manager application. The Explorer and Integrated management functions in the web application are available as a Silverlight component enabling the management process to be easier and faster.

212: How an Entity Member is managed in MDS?
Answer:

The Explorer tool in Master Data Services web application allows adding/modifying the members of an entity. Master Data Services in SQL Server 2012 allows configuring an entity to automatically generate the code value. This automatic generation of code value occurs only when the code value is empty. This code value can be always overridden.

213: What is the new improvement in SQL Server 2012 MDS for many-to-many relationships?
Answer:

SQL Server 2012 MDS gives the ability to use the Explorer to view entities with many-to-many relationships. The relationships between products and parts in MDS can be managed by creating three entities. They are Products, Parts and Entity Mapping. Explore provides the option to open the Related Entities pane that displays Product Code, Parts Code. Furthermore, this entity pane allows viewing the details pane to get the entity member and its attribute values.

214: What is Collection Management and how it is handled in MDS?

Answer:

Collection Management in MDS is a new feature that allows organizing a set of entity members as a collection. This collection management ability assigns a weight to each collection member. MDS allows only storing the weight by subscribing systems that allocates values across the collection members. Hence the subscription view includes the weight column.

215: Explain the staging process steps involved in master data management process.

Answer:

MDS uses a new high performance staging process to load members and attribute values at one time instead of executing in batches. This process loads the data in staging tables. They are:

   a) **stg.name_Leaf:** Table to stage for leaf members and their attributes

   b) **stg.name_Consolidated:** Table to stage for consolidated members and their attributes

   c) **stg.name_Relationship:** Table to assign members in an explicit hierarchy

216: What approaches are available to start a staging process in MDS?

Answer:

The staging process in MDS can be started in two ways. They are:

   a) Integration Management functional area

      i)   Execute the Start Batch operation in Integration management

ii) The status of the execution changes from Queued To Run to Running to Completed

iii) Any Error on data processes can be viewed using query:

SELECT * from [stg].[viw_Product_MemberErrorDetails] WHERE Batch_ID = 1

b) Executing stored procedures

i) Execute the stored procedures corresponding to staging table:

stg.udp_name_Leaf,stg.udp_name_Consolidated, stg.udp_name_Relationship

217: What are the parameters associated with the staging process execution stored procedure?

Answer:

The Staging process execution stored procedure has the following parameters:

a) **VersionName:** Provides version name of the model. The SQL Server database collation setting determines whether the value for this parameter is case sensitive

b) **LogFile:** Set the value as 0 or 1 to disable or enable the log transactions

c) **BatchTag**

i) String to identify the batch in the staging table

ii) It is a string of 50 characters or less

iii) Displays in the batch grid in the Integration Management functional area

218: How User and Group permissions are managed in MDS?

Answer:

MDS provides a "Manage User" page in the web application to manage e User and Group permissions. MDS allows assigning permission by functional area and by model object. Applying permission for a model to a user or group in MDS applies to low level objects. Furthermore, setting permission can be refined on attribute objects. The model permissions object tree including derived and explicit hierarchies are not available in SQL Server 2012 MDS. Instead the derived hierarchy inherits from the model and explicit hierarchy inherits from attribute groups.

219: What are the tools available for Model Deployment?

Answer:

MDS supports two tools for Model Deployment. They are:

a) **Model Deployment Wizard:** A wizard in the MDS web application to deploy the model structure

b) **MDSModelDeploy Tool:** A new high performance, command-line tool to create and deploy a package with model or a package with model objects and data

220: What is the syntax to run the MDSModelDeploy tool in MDS?

Answer:

The syntax for the execution of MDSModelDeploy tool is:

> MDSModelDeploy <commands> [options]

The commands that are available to execute this tool include:

a) **listservices:** Lists all service instances

b) **listmodels:** Lists all models

c) **listversions**: Lists all versions for a specified model

d) **createpackage:** Create a package for a specified model

e) **deployclone:** Create a duplicate of a specified model

f) **deploynew**: Create a new model

g) **deployupdate:** Deploy a model, and update the model version

h) **help:** View usage, options, and examples

221: What is MDS Add-in for Excel?

Answer:

MDS Add-in for Excel is a new user interface option in SQL Server 2012 MDS for managing master data using Microsoft Excel. The MDS administrator can use this interface option to create new object models like entities and load the data into MDS. This MDS Add-in for Excel works with Excel 2007 and Excel 2010.

222: Explain more about Master data management using Add-in for Excel.

Answer:

MDS Add-in for Excel supports all the tasks required to perform the master data management tasks. The tasks include:

a) Create Connection to MDS database

b) Load the data into an Excel sheet from MDS

c) Make changes /additions in bulk

d) Apply business rules

e) Correct the validation issues

   f)   Check duplicates using Data Quality Services Integration

   g)   Publish the modified data back to MDS

223: Explain the behavior of the MDS Add-in for Excel on data refresh.

Answer:

Master data option in the worksheet provides a "Load or Refresh" button to refresh the MDS data without losing the data that has been added in the working sheet. The refresh process updates the contents on the sheet. Here, deleted members disappear and new members appear at the bottom of the table with green highlighting. The cell doesn't change color to identify the new attribute value. It is recommended to publish the changes before refreshing the data in the sheet.

224: How is Data Publication done through the Excel worksheet?

Answer:

Any changes like addition or modification of data or delete members should be followed by Data Publishing to MDS so that it will be available to other users. Data Publishing provides the option to annotate to the document with the reasons for the changes. It also allows providing single annotation for all changes. An annotation should be a short description within 500 characters. Cell comments will be deleted during the publication process from the worksheet. During publication, MDS validates the changes by applying business rules to the data and then confirming the validity of the attribute value.

225: Discuss elaborately about model building in MDS using Add-in for Excel.

Answer:

MDS Add-in for Excel allows the MDS administrator to create entities and add attributes. Here, first it is required to create the model using Master Data Manager and then add entities and attributes using Add-in. It is required to provide the correct data type and length of the attribute after creating the entity as it cannot be changed later. It also provides the Automatic Code generation option for entity members.

226: What are the Domain-based attributes in a worksheet?

Answer:

In an Excel worksheet, restricting column values of an existing entity to a specified set of values can be done by creating a Domain-based attribute. The Attribute properties option of the worksheet provides an option to select a constrained list (Domain-Based) in the attribute type.

227: What is a shortcut query file in MDS?

Answer:

A shortcut query file allows opening and loading frequently accessed data easily. This shortcut file contains:
  a) MDS Database connection details
  b) Model and Version of the MDS data
  c) Filters to apply
  d) Column order

This shortcut query file can be created using a Save Query option in the worksheet. The Save Query option allows sending the file as an email that can be opened easily by the recipient in Microsoft Outlook 2010.

228: How Data Quality Services can be used in MDS?
Answer:
Data Quality Services (DQS) is used to identify the duplicates of data. Before adding a new member in MDS Add-in for Excel, it can be combined with the data in the worksheet for comparison using DQS. DQS integration can be enabled using Master Data Services Configuration Manager and creating a required data matching policy in the knowledge base.

229: Explain the Data-Quality Matching Process in MDS worksheet.
Answer:
The Data Quality Matching process follows as:
   a) Load Data from MDS in first worksheet
   b) Prepare a second worksheet that must contain data with a header row
   c) Combine data from both sheets into single worksheet using Combine Data dialog box in MDS worksheet
   d) Combining data should display the rows of second worksheet into first sheet and the SOURCE column displays the rows is from first or second worksheet
   e) Selecting DQS Knowledge base in Match Data dialog box should map the worksheet columns to a domain

     i)   Adding new rows in this Match Data dialog box for matching requires assigning a weight value

f)   After combing and matching data, the show detail gives the columns containing the matching details. The SCORE column indicates the similarity between the pivot record and the matching record

230: How MDS has been integrated with SharePoint?

Answer:

MDS can be integrated with SharePoint in two ways:

a)   **Adding Master Data Website to SharePoint:** Including andhosted=true as a query parameter the amount of required display space

b)   **Saving a Shortcut Query Files to SharePoint document library:** Provides list of references to other SharePoint users

231: Explain about Bulk Updates and Export in MDS.

Answer:

Making changes in Master data one record is a tedious process and it can be addressed by the following ways:

a)   Use Staging process to load the new values into stg.name_LEAF table

b)   Use MDS Add-in to load into Excel worksheet to update in bulk and then publish the data to MDS

In SQL Server 2012, MDS doesn't provide the option to export to Excel on the Member Information page as the MDS Add-in for Excel can load the data into a worksheet.

232: How are Transactions being used in MDS?

Answer:

MDS uses Transactions to log each and every change that have been made on the master data. In SQL Server 2012 MDS, only administrator can review the transactions in Explorer functional area and can reverse their transaction to return to the original value. MDS allows annotating the Transactions. Though the annotation is associated with transactions, MDS stores the annotation separately and it cannot be deleted.

This page is intentionally left blank.

Chapter 9

Analysis Services and PowerPivot

233: Differentiate between OLAP and OLTP. Is SQL Server Analysis Services (SSAS) the OLAP or OLTP component of SQL?

Answer:

OLAP is On-Line Analytical Processing which is used for generating business intelligence reports using the transactional data available in the database. The Data warehousing module uses OLAP to produce analytical reports based on Reporting Services, MS Excel or some other 3rd party business tools. It is based on these reports and analytics that the management gets a bird's eye view as well as in-depth view of the various transactions happening within the organization. The management takes important decisions based on these reports. OLTP or On-Line Transaction Processing is the day to day transactions that are the base data for these business intelligence reports created using an OLAP component. OLTP contains the most recent transactional data available with very little historical data whereas OLAP relies heavily on the historical data, though a little real-time data will also help. SSAS uses the OLAP component of SQL Server to create cubes that processes and stores complex aggregate data. It also provides valuable information like the patterns, trends etc.

234: Which are the Storage Modes that Cube Partitions support?
Answer:
SSAS basically contains 2 types of data – summary and detailed data. Depending on the method used to store it, there are 3 storage modes supported by the Cube partitions – ROLAP, MOLAP and HOLAP. ROLAP or Real-Time Online analytical Processing stores the summary data in the relational data warehouse and the detailed data in the relational database. Though it can handle a large volume of data and can use the relational database functionalities, the query response time is very slow and it has limited aggregate functions which are required for analytical reports. MOLAP or Multi-Dimensional Online Analytical Processing stores both the summary and detailed data in its data warehousing database or the OLAP server. This makes MOLAP much faster and can work around complex calculations. Since it stores the multidimensional data in Cubes, additional investment in terms of man and machine are required to implement MOLAP. But it still has limitations in handling large volumes of data.

HOLAP or Hybrid Online Analytical Processing is a mix of ROLAP and MOLAP. Here the summary is stored in OLAP Cubes and details are stored in relational data warehouse. It ensures optimal use of storage space, relatively faster query response time and faster processing.

235: Explain the different aggregation functions available in SSAS.

Answer:

SSAS aggregates are summarised values which are stored in the data warehouse which are used to business intelligence reports. SSAS supports 3 types of Aggregation functions such as Fully Additive, Semi-Additive and Non Additive. Fully Additive aggregates are basically a summary of the data like sum or count. Semi-Additive aggregates do not sum up the data, instead returns the specific data from the group such as the FirstChild, LastChild, Min, Max, AverageofChildren, FirstNonEmpty, LastNonEmpty etc. When the aggregate function is set to None it is a Non Additive aggregate. DistinctCount is also a Non Additive aggregate as it will return the number of records that have distinctive value.

236: What are translations? What is its significance in SSAS?

Answer:

In this era of globalisation, translations are an important aspect of any data. When data goes international, people would prefer to see more localised data that are relevant to them and one that they can easily understand. Representing data and interfaces in the

local language everytime can be challenging. The SSAS
translations help us to bind the tags, labels or properties of the
objects that can be represented in different languages. It allows
translation of data and metadata. There are many objects like
cubes, databases, attributes, dimensions, hierarchies, calculated
members, KPIs, measure groups etc. that can be translated in
SSAS.

**237: What are the different server modes in which SQL Server
2012 Analysis Services can execute?**
Answer:
An Analysis Services instance in SQL Server 2012 can be executed
in three server modes. They are:
   a) **Multidimensional:** Uses Analysis Services engine
   b) **PowerPivot for SharePoint:** Uses VertiPaq engine
   c) **Tabular:** Uses its own engine

**238: What type of security is being followed in the different
Analysis Services server modes?**
Answer:
The different levels of security being followed in Analysis Services
server modes are:
   a) Multidimensional server mode uses Security Cell-level
       security
   b) Tabular mode using Row-level security
   c) PowerPivot File-level security using SharePoint
       permissions

239: Name some of the Model Design Features that exist across all the server modes of Analysis Services.

Answer:

Some of the model design features that exist in all server modes of Analysis Services include:

a) **Calculated Measures:** Provides multidimensional tabular support design which gives the sum of other measures

b) **Semi-additive Measures:** Values that summarize across any related dimension except time

c) **Distinct Count:** Used to find the number of distinct count in addition to other aggregations

d) **Hierarchies:** Analysis of data at different levels using logical relationship and allows a user to navigate from one level to another

e) **Parent-Child Hierarchies:** A hierarchy based on two table columns well suited for handling large data

f) **Perspectives:** Displays a subset of model objects when there are many objects in the model so that users can easily find objects they need

240: How is an analysis services project in SQL Server 2012 created?

Answer:

An analysis services project can be created through a tool called SQL Server Data Tools (SSDT). SSDT is a model development tool for multidimensional, tabular and data mining models. An available template in SSDT can be used for creating the analysis services project.

241: How many templates are available for Analysis Services Projects and what are they?

Answer:

There are five templates available for Analysis Services projects. They are:

a) Analysis Services Multidimensional and Data Mining Project

b) Import from Server (Multidimensional and Data Mining)

c) Analysis Services Tabular Project

d) Import from PowerPivot

e) Import from Server (Tabular)

242: What is a tabular model in SQL Server 2012?

Answer:

A tabular model is a new database structure type that is being supported by Analysis Services in SQL Server 2012. Creating a tabular project in SQL Server Data Tool will create a model.bim and a workspace database where the model will be developed by importing data and designing objects.

243: What are the workspace database properties in Model Designer of SQL Server Data Tool?

Answer:

The workspace database properties in Model Designer of SQL Server Data Tool are:

a) **Data Backup:** Data backup setting and the default setting is "Do Not Backup To Disk"

b) **Workspace Database:** Displays the name of the workspace database

c) **Workspace Retention:** Determines whether to keep the workspace database in memory

d) **Workspace Server:** Specifies the server to host the workspace database

244: Explain the Tabular Model Designer.

Answer:

The Tabular Model Designer displays the data imported from data sources in the workspace as rows and columns. It allows the column name to be changed as required. Importing data from relational data sources detects the existing relationships and adds them to the model. Model Designer can highlight the data related columns in each table.

245: How are table relationships managed in model designer?

Answer:

Model Designer allows managing the table relations by providing options to create, edit and delete. New relationship between two tables can be made just by dragging a column in a table over another column in the second table. It is possible to create only one-to-one relationship and one-to-many relationships. Multiple relationships can be created but only one will be active.

246: What is a calculated column in analysis service?

Answer:

A calculated column is a column of data derived using a DAX (Data Analysis Expression) formula. This kind of calculated

column can be created by adding a column defined with a DAX
formula. This formula can be created with the combination of
columns. Model Designer calculates and displays values for all the
rows in the table.

247: Explain the Key Performance Indicators in Analysis service.
Answer:
Key Performance Indicators (KPIs) are a special type of measure
that can be used to measure progress or status. To create a KPI,
define the measure or absolute value representing the target value
of KPI. The status threshold value represents the boundaries
across each level of progress. Analysis Services compares the base
value to the threshold to determine and display KPI Status.

248: What are the different security permission roles available in
the tabular model to perform an action?
Answer:
The tabular model is secure and requires the following permission
to authorize the role members to perform the actions. The role
permissions are:
   a) **Read:** Member can query the data only
   b) **Process**: Member can process the data only
   c) **Read And Process:** Member can query the data and
      execute process operations
   d) **Administrator**: Member has full permissions to query,
      execute and make changes to the model
   e) **None**: Member cannot use the model in any way

249: What are the reporting properties that can be changed on a selected table or column in Model Designer?

Answer:

The table-level changeable reporting properties in Model Designer are:

    a) Default Field Set

    b) Default Image

    c) Default Label

    d) Keep Unique Rows

    e) Row Identifier

The column-level changeable reporting properties for a table in Model Designer are:

    a) Default Label

    b) Image URL

    c) Row Identifier

    d) Table Detail Position

250: Compare the model behavior for different available features in In-memory and Direct-Query modes.

Answer:

The following table lists the features in In-memory and Direct-Query mode:

Features	In-memory mode	Direct-Query mode
Data sources	Relational database, Analysis Services, Reporting Services report, Excel & Text files	SQL Server 2005 or later
Calculations	Measures, KPIs, Calculated columns	Measures, KPIs
DAX	Fully functional	Time intelligence functions invalid, statistical functions evaluate differently
Security	Analysis Services roles	SQL Server permissions

251: What are the new features of the Multidimensional model storage in SQL Server 2012 Analysis Services?

Answer:

MOLAP engine now uses a new type of storage for string data. Set "StringStoreCompatibilityLevel" to 1100 in SQL Server Data Tool's Dimension designer; this makes Analysis Services load the data into the new string store. Although the file size limitation is gone, the file can contain only 4 billion unique strings or 4 billion records.

252: Explain Event tracing in Analysis Services.

Answer:

The SQL Server Extended Events Framework is used to capture any Analysis Services event. Creating a XMLA (XML for Analysis) script enables the tracing of specific events like Query Subcube, Get Data from Aggregation/Cache, Query End events. In SQL Server 2012, there are new events available such as: Lock Required, Lock Waiting, Lock Acquired, Lock Released and Lock Timeout. There are events available to monitor the Server modes such as: VertiPaq SE Query Begin/End and Direct Query Begin/End events.

253: What are XMLA Schema Rowsets?

Answer:

New schema rowsets are available to explore the metadata of a model and to monitor the Analysis Services server. The following schema rowsets can be queried by using Dynamic Management Views for VertiPaq engines and tabular models:

a) **DISCOVER_CALC_DEPENDENCY:** Finds dependencies between columns, measures and formulas

b) **DISCOVER_CSDL_METADATA:** Retrieves the Conceptual Schema Definition Language for tabular model

c) **DISCOVER_XEVENT_TRACE_DEFINITION:** Monitors SQL Server Extended Events

d) **DISCOVER_TRACES:** Uses the new column, Type, to filter traces by category

e) **MDSCHEMA_HIERARCHIES:** Uses the new column, Structure_Type, to filter hierarchies

254: What configurations need to be specified to deploy an Analysis Services instances in NUMA architecture?

Answer:

To deploy Analysis Services instances in NUMA architecture or in more than 64 processors, the following instance properties need to be configured:

a) **Thread pools:** Assign each process, IO process, query, parsing, and VertiPag thread pool to a separate processor group

b) **Affinity masks:** Use the processor group affinity mask to include or exclude an instance in a processor group

c) **Memory allocation:** Specify memory ranges to assign to processor groups

255: What is PowerPivot for Excel and what are its benefits?

Answer:

PowerPivot for Excel is a client application/Excel add-on that incorporates SQL Server data into the Excel workspace. This workspace opens over Excel and can build analytical databases inside the Excel. The VertiPaq Engine runs over Excel and handles the data loading and compression. This provides data visualization in an Excel worksheet.

256: What is PowerPivot for SharePoint and what are its benefits?

Answer:

PowerPivot for SharePoint provides hosting of PowerPivot the analytical data model in a SharePoint server farm. Hosting the PowerPivot data in SharePoint gives centralized data access and shared service. Administration and managing PowerPivot data can be easily done as it uses the SharePoint farm properties.

257: Describe the installation and configuration dependencies associated with PowerPivot for SharePoint.

Answer:

Installing PowerPivot for SharePoint within the SharePoint Server farm has many dependencies. They are:

a) Install SharePoint Server 2010 and SharePoint Server 2010

Service Pack 1 before installing PowerPivot for SharePoint

b) Use the PowerPivot Configuration tool and complete the configuration of SharePoint farm and PowerPivot for SharePoint as a single process

c) To run optimally, monitor and ensure that the server supports its workload.

258: What are the properties required to manage the cache in Management Dashboard?

Answer:

The configuration properties that are required to manage the cache include:

a) **Keep Inactive Database In Memory:** Analysis Services keeps a workbook in memory for 48 hours following the last query. This value can be decreased if necessary

b) **Keep Inactive Database In Cache:** After Analysis Services releases a workbook from memory, the workbook persists in cache and consumes disk space for 120 hours; this value can also be reduced

259: What are the settings associated with health rules of Analysis Services and what are its default values?

Answer:

Setting	Description	Default Value
Insufficient CPU Resource Allocation	Triggers warning message when CPU utilization is more than specified percentage	80%
Insufficient CPU Resources On The System	Triggers warning message when CPU usage of the server is more than specified percentage	90%
Insufficient Memory Threshold	Triggers memory warning message when the available memory is lower than the memory allocated to Analysis Services	5%
Maximum Number of Connections	Triggers warning message when the number of connections exceeds the specified number.	100
Insufficient Disk Space	Triggers warning message when the available disk space for the backup folder falls below the specified value	5%
Data Collection Interval	Defines the period of time for the server level health rules to apply	4 hours

260: What is a Data Refresh configuration in Analysis Services?

Answer:

Data Refresh operation refreshes the data for the active workbook. This operation consumes more server resource and hence it should be deactivated if not required. The following configuration settings are available for data refresh:

a) **Disable Data Refresh Due To Consecutive Failures:** For this consecutive number of failure times, PowerPivot service application deactivates the data-refresh schedule. Default value is 10

b) **Disable Data Refresh For Inactive Workbooks:** The specified number of data-refresh cycles executed on inactive workbook. Default value is 10; setting value to 0 keeps the data refresh active

261: What are the Analysis services functionalities that have been discontinued in SQL Server 2012?

Answer:

There are two Analysis services functionalities that have been discontinued in SQL Server 2012. They are:

a) **Migration Wizard:** Used to migrate legacy SQL Server Analysis Services database into new version

b) **DSO Library:** Decision Support Object (DSO) Library that provided compatibility with earlier version of analysis services

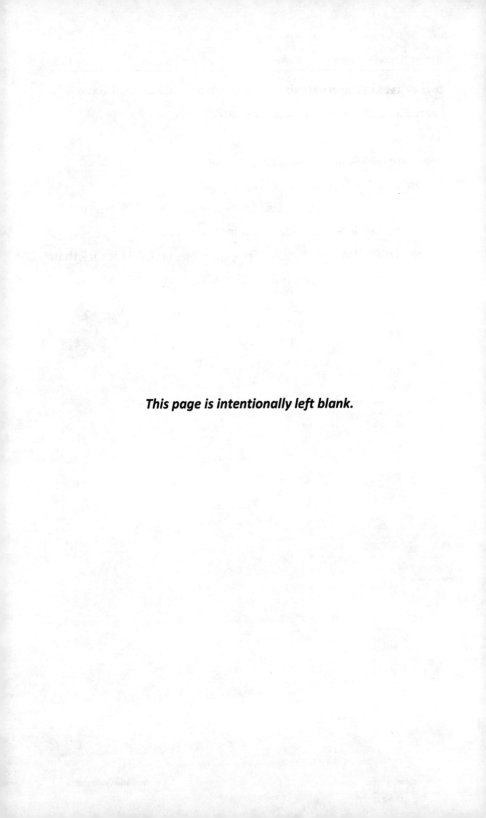
This page is intentionally left blank.

Chapter 10

Reporting Services

262: Explain the SQL Server Reporting Services and its components.

Answer:

The SQL Reporting Services contain the different components and services used to create, organize and handle business intelligence reports for the organization. It also helps you to create customized reports exclusively for specific purposes that help decision-making. Reporting services lets the user create interactive reports in tabular or graphical forms from relational, multi-dimensional or XML data sources. It is a server-based platform which is integrated with the SQL server components and tools. There's a variety of formats available for viewing and exporting which can be made available on web based applications also. There are 3 components in SSRS – the Report Designer which helps us to create the reports, the Report Server which helps to execute and publish the reports and the Report Manager which helps to manage the Report Server.

263: List out the advantages of using SSRS.

Answer:

The SSRS is a fast and cheap way to create, publish and manage business intelligence reports. It can efficiently access the data from SQL Server and Oracle Databases. It is easy to use and hence does not require specially trained users. Since the report designer is available in Visual Studio .Net, it can be used to create the reports also along with the applications in the same environment. It is well secured. We just need to specify the parameters for the reports and the User Interface to accept these parameters is automatically created. Reports that are subscribed to are automatically sent as emails to the users.

264: List out the limitations in the SQL Server express edition of SSRS.

Answer:

Though SSRS comes as a free installable component with SQL Server, the Express Edition of Reporting Server has some reported issues. The first and foremost issue is the IDE, Management Studio cannot be used for administration of report server. There are not report models available and report builder is also not available. We cannot cache the reports as in Crystal Server. The reports' history and delivery also are not available. There's no SQL server agent for SSRS. We cannot schedule using report server. Only local SQL server can be used for retrieving and storing Report Data. Rendering is possible only using Excel, PDF and Image formats. The maximum RAM usage allowed is 1 GB. It does not allow any subscription and cannot be integrated with Sharepoint. We cannot implement role based security features. It supports only named instances.

265: What are the Types of SSRS?

Answer:

SSRS allows the users to create a variety of reports based on the data available in the internal or external data source. We can create Parameterized reports wherein the user can input or set the parameters such as the From and To dates for which the report has to be generated. Linked reports can be created which will be based on existing reports. It will have the base report's layout and data source though the security, subscriptions, parameters etc. can be different. A Snapshot report is a report which is created at a pre-determined period of time and is already available in the reporting server. It is just displayed as required in a portable format though it does not contain the real-time data.   Cached reports are saved copies of processed reports. Clickthrough reports are the interactive reports that lets the user generate a report and then clicking on a particular parameter takes the user to another report. Drilldown reports contain a large amount of data that is shown in an aggregate and then based on the user requirement, can be drilled down to the details. Drillthrough reports are reports generated when the user clicks on a link or text box in the main summary report to display the details of the particular parameter. It is generated only on demand. Subreports are smaller reports with related data that are included within the main report.

266: What are the core features of the Reporting Services in SQL Server from its inception?

Answer:

Reporting Services was introduced in Microsoft SQL Server 2000 and its core features includes:

a) Services to manage reporting functionality from different data stores

b) Viewing reports in variety of formats like Excel sheet, Windows application, or SharePoint sites

c) Programming features to customize the reporting as per user requirement

267: What are the improvements available in SQL Server 2012 reporting services?

Answer:

SQL Server 2012 reporting services includes the following improvements:

a) A new architecture in SharePoint integration mode allowing it to be configured as a SharePoint service application

b) Power View provides expanded data visualization and self service capabilities

c) Data Alert Management System sends email for the specified condition on report data in SharePoint integration mode

268: What are the new renderers added to SQL Server 2012 reporting services?

Answer:

The two new renderers added in SQL Server 2012 reporting services are:

a) **Excel 2010 Renderer:** Produces reports as XLSX file in Open Office Excel format that can hold a maximum number of rows and columns

b) **Word 2010 Renderer:** Generates report as DOCX file that uses a compression to generate a smaller file

269: What are the benefits of the new SharePoint Shared service architecture in SQL Server 2012 reporting services?

Answer:

The benefits of the SharePoint Shared service architecture in SQL Server 2012 reporting services include:

a) Better Performance and Scalability in the administration and configuration process

b) Reporting services across web applications

c) Uses SharePoint for backup and recovery process

d) Uses claims-based authentication to control access

270: Explain the Service Application Configuration.

Answer:

The Service Application configuration in SQL Server 2012 reporting service doesn't require Reporting Service Settings to configure; instead it should be configured through the SharePoint Central Administration interface.

The steps to create the Service Application include:

a) Specify the application pool identifier under which Reporting service runs

b) Create 3 report server data bases

    i) First database for storing server and catalog data

    ii) Second for caching data sets/reports

    iii) Third for data alert management

c) Configure settings for Reporting services

d) Access Manage Service Applications in Central Administration for updating the credentials

271: What is a Power View?

Answer:

Power View is a self-service feature in Reporting service. The advantage of this View includes:

a) A browser based Silver-light application that runs Reporting services in SharePoint integration mode

b) Instead of designing and previewing using a Designer, it allows to directly work with data in the presentation layout

272: What are the data source types available with Power View?

Answer:

There are three data source types available to use with Power View:

a) **PowerPivot Workbook:** A workbook from PowerPivot Gallery as a source

b) **Shared data source:** Using Reporting Services Shared Data

Source (RSDS) file

c) **Business Intelligence Semantic Model (BISM)
Connection file:** BISM file to connect to PowerPivot
workbook or to an Analysis Services tabular model

**273: What are the options available to open a Power View
Design environment for creating a new report?**

Answer:

There are two ways the Power View Design environment can be
opened for creating a new report:

a) **PowerPivot Workbook:** Use the Create Power View
Report option in Workbook that displays in PowerPivot
Gallery

b) **Data Connection Library:** Use the Create Power View
Report option in BISM or RSDS file

274: Explain the Power View Design environment.

Answer:

Power View Design environment creates a blank view workspace
to create the report. Tables and Data visualizations can be added
over the view workspace. The view size is fixed in height and
width. If more space is required, then add more views and
navigate between views. The field list section in the environment
gives the list of table names of the model.

**275: How are tabular model field lists represented in the
Reporting Service Power View design environment?**

Answer:

The tabular model should be expanded in the Power View Design environment to view the field lists. It contains the following items:

a) **Individual field:** No icon

b) **Row label field:** Identifies the column configured with the reporting properties in the model; represented with a gray and white icon

c) **Calculated column:** A sigma icon

d) **Measures:** A calculator icon

276: What Data Visualization is available in Power View?

Answer:

Data Visualization allows viewing the required table data in visual format. A table is the only way to explore data in Power View. The different types of visualization include:

a) **Matrix:** Provides the explored data in table format

b) **Charts:** Allows visualizing data along the axis

c) **Cards and Tiles:** Allows visualizing the list of data in Card format

277: Explain about the different types of Chart Visualizations.

Answer:

In the Power View Design environment, adding a "Measure" to the table enables Chart Visualizations. The different types of Chart Visualization include - Column, Bar, Line and Scatter charts. The Design environment allows resizing, add/remove fields to visualize. The Layout section in Power View allows adding chart title, data label and legends.

278: How to work with overlapping visualizations in Charts?

Answer:

The Chart Visualization can have overlap and inset items. The Home tab of the ribbon in the Power View provides a way to arrange the chart using an Arrange button by moving an item forward or back. To view an item in isolation, the Power View provides option to fill the entire view within the selected visualization.

279: Explain more about Card visualization in Charts.

Answer:

Card visualization is a scrollable list of grouped fields arranged in a card format. Here, the default label and default image fields are more prominent and featured. The size of the card changes dynamically on adding/removing the table fields. This can be controlled using Sizing Handle in Card container. It allows changing the sequence of fields by rearranging items.

280: What is a Tile Visualization in Charts?

Answer:

A Tile Visualization is a display that filters a collection of cards that has the same value. There are two default tiles layout available in Power View - Tab-strip mode and cover-flow mode. These two layout modes are differentiated based on the positioning of label or image and the selected value being displayed. The tile container allows converting a table or matrix directly to a tile.

281: How is play axis used in Scatter chart and Bubble chart?

Answer:

Scatter chart contains two measures associated with the chart - one for horizontal axis and another for vertical axis. Bubble chart contains three measures - the third measure to represent size in the chart. With the play axis defined, it allows displaying the visualization in sequence for each value that appears on the play axis.

282: What is "Multiples" in Charts?

Answer:

"Multiples" allows viewing the data by breaking the chart into multiple copies. Power View design creates separate charts in Vertical Multiples and in Horizontal Multiples area. It allows selecting a number of tiles across and down to include. If visualization has more tiles than grid length, then a scrollable chart appears to access all the tiles.

283: Elaborate on Power View Filter.

Answer:

View Filter defines the filter criteria on the current view. Every view will have its own set of filters associated with it. Adding a new filter in default mode requires dragging a field to the Filter area in Power View followed by selecting the required value. Advanced filter criteria provides more flexible filter criteria. Some of the advanced filter criteria include:

    a)   Filtering on string data type allows filtering with operators like contains, starts with

b) Filtering on numeric data type allows filtering with operators like greater than, less than

c) Filtering on date allows operators like Before, After

The Visualization filter allows configuring the filter for a selected visualization.

284: What are the display modes available in Power View?

Answer:

There are three display modes available in Power view for easy navigation between views:

a) **Fit to Window:** View shrinks or expands to fill the available space in the window

b) **Reading Mode:** Only the Power View browser tab and button will be visible with multi-view button to navigate

c) **Full Screen Mode:** Similar to full screen presentation using PPT

285: How are created reports exported in Power View?

Answer:

Power View provides the ability to export the created reports to Power Point as a PPTX file. In this report, each view will become a separate slide and the view content will be available as a static image. If your presentation has an active connection/permission with the report in SharePoint report, then editing the presentation slide will take it to Power view.

286: What are the features of Data Alerts?

Answer:

Data Alerts refer to defining an alert notification on the data when the specific condition on the data is true. This self service feature is new to SQL Server 2012 Reporting service and will be available with SharePoint integrated mode. Data alert works with the reports created with Report Designer or Builder. It doesn't work with the Power View reports.

287: What is the process followed for Data Alert Creation?
Answer:
The Data Alert Creation process follows as:
   a) Define rules for data region in the report using Data Alert Designer
   b) Specify the recurring schedule that evaluates the defined rules
   c) Configure the email settings for generating the email
   d) Save the defined rules; in turn, reporting service will save the rule in Alert Database and schedules a SQL Server Agent Job

288: How does the Alerting service process the data alerts?
Answer:
The Alerting service in Reporting service manages the process of refreshing the data feed. While refreshing the data, it applies the rules in the data alert definitions. Then the alerting service creates an alerting instance to record the process. During this process, if the defined rule is satisfied with the data feed, the alert service will generate an email with the result to the configured recipient email address. If the process execution results in error, the alerting

services will send the error message to the configured recipient email address.

289: What are the Alert configuration settings and their default values?

Answer:

The Alert configuration settings are available in the RsReportServer.config file and its settings are manually edited as there is no interface available.

Configuration Setting	Default Value
AlertingCleanupCyclingMinutes	20
AlertingExecutionLogCleanupMinutes	10080
AlertingDataCleanupMinutes	360
AlertingMaxDataRetentionDays	180
IsAlertingService	TRUE

290: What are the Alert Service events that are supported for all alerts?

Answer:

The following Alert Service features are supported:

a) **GenerateAlert:** This processes the data feed, rules, and alert instances

b) **DeliverAlert:** This Creates Message and Deliver

c) **FireAlert:** This is an On-demand execution of an alert

d) **CreateSchedule:** This Creates schedule as defined in data alert

e) **UpdateSchedule:** This provides option to Modify the schedule

f) **DeleteSchedule:** This Deletes a schedule

g) **FireSchedule:** This is the scheduled execution of an alert

This page is intentionally left blank.

HR Questions

Review these typical interview questions and think about how you would answer them. Read the answers listed; you will find best possible answers along with strategies and suggestions.

1: How would you handle a negative coworker?

Answer:

Everyone has to deal with negative coworkers – and the single best way to do so is to remain positive. You may try to build a relationship with the coworker or relate to them in some way, but even if your efforts are met with a cold shoulder, you must retain your positive attitude. Above all, stress that you would never allow a coworker's negativity to impact your own work or productivity.

2: What would you do if you witnessed a coworker surfing the web, reading a book, etc, wasting company time?

Answer:

The interviewer will want to see that you realize how detrimental it is for employees to waste company time, and that it is not something you take lightly. Explain the way you would adhere to company policy, whether that includes talking to the coworker yourself, reporting the behavior straight to a supervisor, or talking to someone in HR.

3: How do you handle competition among yourself and other employees?

Answer:

Healthy competition can be a great thing, and it is best to stay focused on the positive aspects of this here. Don't bring up conflict among yourself and other coworkers, and instead focus on the motivation to keep up with the great work of others, and the ways in which coworkers may be a great support network in helping to push you to new successes.

4: When is it okay to socialize with coworkers?

Answer:

This question has two extreme answers (all the time, or never), and your interviewer, in most cases, will want to see that you fall somewhere in the middle. It's important to establish solid relationships with your coworkers, but never at the expense of getting work done. Ideally, relationship-building can happen with exercises of teamwork and special projects, as well as in the break room.

5: Tell me about a time when a major change was made at your last job, and how you handled it.

Answer:

Provide a set-up for the situation including the old system, what the change was, how it was implemented, and the results of the change, and include how you felt about each step of the way. Be sure that your initial thoughts on the old system are neutral, and that your excitement level grows with each step of the new change, as an interviewer will be pleased to see your adaptability.

6: When delegating tasks, how do you choose which tasks go to which team members?

Answer:

The interviewer is looking to gain insight into your thought process with this question, so be sure to offer thorough reasoning behind your choice. Explain that you delegate tasks based on each individual's personal strengths, or that you look at how many other projects each person is working on at the time, in order to create the best fit possible.

7: Tell me about a time when you had to stand up for something you believed strongly about to coworkers or a supervisor.
Answer:
While it may be difficult to explain a situation of conflict to an interviewer, this is a great opportunity to display your passions and convictions, and your dedication to your beliefs. Explain not just the situation to the interviewer, but also elaborate on why it was so important to you to stand up for the issue, and how your coworker or supervisor responded to you afterward – were they more respectful? Unreceptive? Open-minded? Apologetic?

8: Tell me about a time when you helped someone finish their work, even though it wasn't "your job."
Answer:
Though you may be frustrated when required to pick up someone else's slack, it's important that you remain positive about lending a hand. The interviewer will be looking to see if you're a team player, and by helping someone else finish a task that he or she couldn't manage alone, you show both your willingness to help the team succeed, and your own competence.

9: What are the challenges of working on a team? How do you handle this?
Answer:

There are many obvious challenges to working on a team, such as handling different perspectives, navigating individual schedules, or accommodating difficult workers. It's best to focus on one challenge, such as individual team members missing deadlines or failing to keep commitments, and then offer a solution that clearly addresses the problem. For example, you could organize weekly status meetings for your team to discuss progress, or assign shorter deadlines in order to keep the long-term deadline on schedule.

10: Do you value diversity in the workplace?
Answer:

Diversity is important in the workplace in order to foster an environment that is accepting, equalizing, and full of different perspectives and backgrounds. Be sure to show your awareness of these issues, and stress the importance of learning from others' experiences.

11: How would you handle a situation in which a coworker was not accepting of someone else's diversity?
Answer:

Explain that it is important to adhere to company policies regarding diversity, and that you would talk to the relevant supervisors or management team. When it is appropriate, it could also be best to talk to the coworker in question about the benefits of alternate perspectives – if you can handle the situation yourself, it's best not to bring resolvable issues to management.

12: Are you rewarded more from working on a team, or accomplishing a task on your own?

Answer:

It's best to show a balance between these two aspects – your employer wants to see that you're comfortable working on your own, and that you can complete tasks efficiently and well without assistance. However, it's also important for your employer to see that you can be a team player, and that you understand the value that multiple perspectives and efforts can bring to a project.

13: Tell me about a time when you didn't meet a deadline.

Answer:

Ideally, this hasn't happened – but if it has, make sure you use a minor example to illustrate the situation, emphasize how long ago it happened, and be sure that you did as much as you could to ensure that the deadline was met. Additionally, be sure to include what you learned about managing time better or prioritizing tasks in order to meet all future deadlines.

14: How do you eliminate distractions while working?

Answer:

With the increase of technology and the ease of communication, new distractions arise every day. Your interviewer will want to see that you are still able to focus on work, and that your productivity has not been affected, by an example showing a routine you employ in order to stay on task.

15: Tell me about a time when you worked in a position with a

weekly or monthly quota to meet. How often were you successful?

Answer:

Your numbers will speak for themselves, and you must answer this question honestly. If you were regularly met your quotas, be sure to highlight this in a confident manner and don't be shy in pointing out your strengths in this area. If your statistics are less than stellar, try to point out trends in which they increased toward the end of your employment, and show reflection as to ways you can improve in the future.

16: Tell me about a time when you met a tough deadline, and how you were able to complete it.

Answer:

Explain how you were able to prioritize tasks, or to delegate portions of an assignments to other team members, in order to deal with a tough deadline. It may be beneficial to specify why the deadline was tough – make sure it's clear that it was not a result of procrastination on your part. Finally, explain how you were able to successfully meet the deadline, and what it took to get there in the end.

17: How do you stay organized when you have multiple projects on your plate?

Answer:

The interviewer will be looking to see that you can manage your time and work well – and being able to handle multiple projects at once, and still giving each the attention it deserves, is a great mark of a worker's competence and efficiency. Go through a typical process of goal-setting and prioritizing, and explain the steps of these to the interviewer, so he or she can see how well you manage time.

18: How much time during your work day do you spend on "auto-pilot?"

Answer:

While you may wonder if the employer is looking to see how efficient you are with this question (for example, so good at your job that you don't have to think about it), but in almost every case, the employer wants to see that you're constantly thinking, analyzing, and processing what's going on in the workplace. Even if things are running smoothly, there's usually an opportunity somewhere to make things more efficient or to increase sales or productivity. Stress your dedication to ongoing development, and convey that being on "auto-pilot" is not conducive to that type of success.

19: How do you handle deadlines?

Answer:

The most important part of handling tough deadlines is to prioritize tasks and set goals for completion, as well as to delegate or eliminate unnecessary work. Lead the interviewer through a general scenario, and display your competency through your ability to organize and set priorities, and most importantly, remain calm.

20: Tell me about your personal problem-solving process.

Answer:

Your personal problem-solving process should include outlining the problem, coming up with possible ways to fix the problem, and setting a clear action plan that leads to resolution. Keep your answer brief and organized, and explain the steps in a concise, calm manner that shows you are level-headed even under stress.

21: What sort of things at work can make you stressed?

Answer:

As it's best to stay away from negatives, keep this answer brief and simple. While answering that nothing at work makes you stressed will not be very believable to the interviewer, keep your answer to one generic principle such as when members of a team don't keep their commitments, and then focus on a solution you generally employ to tackle that stress, such as having weekly status meetings or intermittent deadlines along the course of a project.

22: What do you look like when you are stressed about something? How do you solve it?

Answer:

This is a trick question – your interviewer wants to hear that you don't look any different when you're stressed, and that you don't allow negative emotions to interfere with your productivity. As far as how you solve your stress, it's best if you have a simple solution mastered, such as simply taking deep breaths and counting to 10 to bring yourself back to the task at hand.

23: Can you multi-task?

Answer:

Some people can, and some people can't. The most important part of multi-tasking is to keep a clear head at all times about what needs to be done, and what priority each task falls under. Explain how you evaluate tasks to determine priority, and how you manage your time in order to ensure that all are completed efficiently.

24: How many hours per week do you work?

Answer:

Many people get tricked by this question, thinking that answering more hours is better – however, this may cause an employer to wonder why you have to work so many hours in order to get the work done that other people can do in a shorter amount of time. Give a fair estimate of hours that it should take you to complete a job, and explain that you are also willing to work extra whenever needed.

25: How many times per day do you check your email?

Answer:

While an employer wants to see that you are plugged into modern technology, it is also important that the number of times you check your email per day is relatively low – perhaps two to three times per day (dependent on the specific field you're in). Checking email is often a great distraction in the workplace, and while it is important to remain connected, much correspondence can simply be handled together in the morning and afternoon.

26: Tell me about a time when you worked additional hours to finish a project.

Answer:

It's important for your employer to see that you are dedicated to your work, and willing to put in extra hours when required or when a job calls for it. However, be careful when explaining why you were called to work additional hours – for instance, did you have to stay late because you set goals poorly earlier in the process? Or on a more positive note, were you working additional hours because a client requested for a deadline to be moved up on short notice? Stress your competence and willingness to give 110% every time.

27: Tell me about a time when your performance exceeded the duties and requirements of your job.

Answer:

If you're a great candidate for the position, this should be an easy question to answer – choose a time when you truly went above and beyond the call of duty, and put in additional work or voluntarily took on new responsibilities. Remain humble, and express gratitude for the learning opportunity, as well as confidence in your ability to give a repeat performance.

28: What is your driving attitude about work?

Answer:

There are many possible good answers to this question, and the interviewer primarily wants to see that you have a great passion for the job and that you will remain motivated in your career if hired. Some specific driving forces behind your success may include hard work, opportunity, growth potential, or success.

29: Do you take work home with you?
Answer:

It is important to first clarify that you are always willing to take work home when necessary, but you want to emphasize as well that it has not been an issue for you in the past. Highlight skills such as time management, goal-setting, and multi-tasking, which can all ensure that work is completed at work.

30: Describe a typical work day to me.
Answer:

There are several important components in your typical work day, and an interviewer may derive meaning from any or all of them, as well as from your ability to systematically lead him or her through the day. Start at the beginning of your day and proceed chronologically, making sure to emphasize steady productivity, time for review, goal-setting, and prioritizing, as well as some additional time to account for unexpected things that may arise.

31: Tell me about a time when you went out of your way at your previous job.
Answer:

Here it is best to use a specific example of the situation that required you to go out of your way, what your specific position would have required that you did, and how you went above that. Use concrete details, and be sure to include the results, as well as reflection on what you learned in the process.

32: Are you open to receiving feedback and criticisms on your job performance, and adjusting as necessary?

Answer:

This question has a pretty clear answer – yes – but you'll need to display a knowledge as to why this is important. Receiving feedback and criticism is one thing, but the most important part of that process is to then implement it into your daily work. Keep a good attitude, and express that you always appreciate constructive feedback.

33: What inspires you?

Answer:

You may find inspiration in nature, reading success stories, or mastering a difficult task, but it's important that your inspiration is positively-based and that you're able to listen and tune into it when it appears. Keep this answer generally based in the professional world, but where applicable, it may stretch a bit into creative exercises in your personal life that, in turn, help you in achieving career objectives.

34: How do you inspire others?

Answer:

This may be a difficult question, as it is often hard to discern the effects of inspiration in others. Instead of offering a specific example of a time when you inspired someone, focus on general principles such as leading by example that you employ in your professional life. If possible, relate this to a quality that someone who inspired you possessed, and discuss the way you have modified or modeled it in your own work.

35: How do you make decisions?
Answer:
This is a great opportunity for you to wow your interviewer with your decisiveness, confidence, and organizational skills. Make sure that you outline a process for decision-making, and that you stress the importance of weighing your options, as well as in trusting intuition. If you answer this question skillfully and with ease, your interviewer will trust in your capability as a worker.

36: What are the most difficult decisions for you to make?
Answer:
Explain your relationship to decision-making, and a general synopsis of the process you take in making choices. If there is a particular type of decision that you often struggle with, such as those that involve other people, make sure to explain why that type of decision is tough for you, and how you are currently engaged in improving your skills.

37: When making a tough decision, how do you gather information?
Answer:
If you're making a tough choice, it's best to gather information from as many sources as possible. Lead the interviewer through your process of taking information from people in different areas,

starting first with advice from experts in your field, feedback from coworkers or other clients, and by looking analytically at your own past experiences.

38: Tell me about a decision you made that did not turn out well.
Answer:

Honesty and transparency are great values that your interviewer will appreciate – outline the choice you made, why you made it, the results of your poor decision – and finally (and most importantly!) what you learned from the decision. Give the interviewer reason to trust that you wouldn't make a decision like that again in the future.

39: Are you able to make decisions quickly?
Answer:

You may be able to make decisions quickly, but be sure to communicate your skill in making sound, thorough decisions as well. Discuss the importance of making a decision quickly, and how you do so, as well as the necessity for each decision to first be well-informed.

40: Ten years ago, what were your career goals?
Answer:

In reflecting back to what your career goals were ten years ago, it's important to show the ways in which you've made progress in that time. Draw distinct links between specific objectives that you've achieved, and speak candidly about how it felt to reach those goals. Remain positive, upbeat, and growth-oriented, even if you haven't yet achieved all of the goals you set out to reach.

41: Tell me about a weakness you used to have, and how you changed it.

Answer:

Choose a non-professional weakness that you used to have, and outline the process you went through in order to grow past it. Explain the weakness itself, why it was problematic, the action steps you planned, how you achieved them, and the end result.

42: Tell me about your goal-setting process.

Answer:

When describing your goal-setting process, clearly outline the way that you create an outline for yourself. It may be helpful to offer an example of a particular goal you've set in the past, and use this as a starting point to guide the way you created action steps, check-in points, and how the goal was eventually achieved.

43: Tell me about a time when you solved a problem by creating actionable steps to follow.

Answer:

This question will help the interviewer to see how you talented you are in outlining, problem resolution, and goal-setting. Explain thoroughly the procedure of outlining the problem, establishing steps to take, and then how you followed the steps (such as through check-in points along the way, or intermediary goals).

44: Where do you see yourself five years from now?

Answer:

Have some idea of where you would like to have advanced to in the position you're applying for, over the next several years. Make sure that your future plans line up with you still working for the company, and stay positive about potential advancement. Focus on future opportunities, and what you're looking forward to – but make sure your reasons for advancement are admirable, such as greater experience and the chance to learn, rather than simply being out for a higher salary.

45: When in a position, do you look for opportunities to promote?

Answer:

There's a fine balance in this question – you want to show the interviewer that you have initiative and motivation to advance in your career, but not at the expense of appearing opportunistic or selfishly-motivated. Explain that you are always open to growth opportunities, and very willing to take on new responsibilities as your career advances.

46: On a scale of 1 to 10, how successful has your life been?

Answer:

Though you may still have a long list of goals to achieve, it's important to keep this answer positively-focused. Choose a high number between 7 and 9, and explain that you feel your life has been largely successful and satisfactory as a result of several specific achievements or experiences. Don't go as high as a 10, as the interviewer may not believe your response or in your ability to reason critically.

47: What is your greatest goal in life?
Answer:
It's okay for this answer to stray a bit into your personal life, but best if you can keep it professionally-focused. While specific goals are great, if your personal goal doesn't match up exactly with one of the company's objectives, you're better off keeping your goal a little more generic and encompassing, such as "success in my career" or "leading a happy and fulfilling life." Keep your answer brief, and show a decisive nature – most importantly, make it clear that you've already thought about this question and know what you want.

48: Tell me about a time when you set a goal in your personal life and achieved it.
Answer:
The interviewer can see that you excel at setting goals in your professional life, but he or she also wants to know that you are consistent in your life and capable of setting goals outside of the office as well. Use an example such as making a goal to eat more healthily or to drink more water, and discuss what steps you outlined to achieve your goal, the process of taking action, and the final results as well.

49: What is your greatest goal in your career?
Answer:

Have a very specific goal of something you want to achieve in your career in mind, and be sure that it's something the position clearly puts you in line to accomplish. Offer the goal as well as your plans to get there, and emphasize clear ways in which this position will be an opportunity to work toward the goal.

50: Tell me about a time when you achieved a goal.

Answer:

Start out with how you set the goal, and why you chose it. Then, take the interviewer through the process of outlining the goal, taking steps to achieve it, the outcome, and finally, how you felt after achieving it or recognition you received. The most important part of this question includes the planning and implementation of strategies, so focus most of your time on explaining these aspects. However, the preliminary decisions and end results are also important, so make sure to include them as well.

51: What areas of your work would you still like to improve in? What are your plans to do this?

Answer:

While you may not want the interviewer to focus on things you could improve on, it's important to be self-aware of your own growth opportunities. More importantly, you can impress an interviewer by having specific goals and actions outlined in order to facilitate your growth, even if your area of improvement is something as simple as increasing sales or finding new ways to create greater efficiency.

52: What is customer service?

Answer:

Customer service can be many things – and the most important consideration in this question is that you have a creative answer. Demonstrate your ability to think outside the box by offering a confident answer that goes past a basic definition, and that shows you have truly considered your own individual view of what it means to take care of your customers. The thoughtful consideration you hold for customers will speak for itself.

53: Tell me about a time when you went out of your way for a customer.

Answer:

It's important that you offer an example of a time you truly went out of your way – be careful not to confuse something that felt like a big effort on your part, with something your employer would expect you to do anyway. Offer an example of the customer's problems, what you did to solve it, and the way the customer responded after you took care of the situation.

54: How do you gain confidence from customers?

Answer:

This is a very open-ended question that allows you to show your customer service skills to the interviewer. There are many possible answers, and it is best to choose something that you've had great experience with, such as "by handling situations with transparency," "offering rewards," or "focusing on great communication." Offer specific examples of successes you've had.

55: Tell me about a time when a customer was upset or agitated – how did you handle the situation?

Answer:

Similarly to handling a dispute with another employee, the most important part to answering this question is to first set up the scenario, offer a step-by-step guide to your particular conflict resolution style, and end by describing the way the conflict was resolved. Be sure that in answering questions about your own conflict resolution style, that you emphasize the importance of open communication and understanding from both parties, as well as a willingness to reach a compromise or other solution.

56: When can you make an exception for a customer?

Answer:

Exceptions for customers can generally be made when in accordance with company policy or when directed by a supervisor. Display an understanding of the types of situations in which an exception should be considered, such as when a customer has endured a particular hardship, had a complication with an order, or at a request.

57: What would you do in a situation where you were needed by both a customer and your boss?

Answer:

While both your customer and your boss have different needs of you and are very important to your success as a worker, it is always best to try to attend to your customer first – however, the key is explaining to your boss why you are needed urgently by the customer, and then to assure your boss that you will attend to his or her needs as soon as possible (unless it's absolutely an urgent matter).

58: What is the most important aspect of customer service?
Answer:
While many people would simply state that customer satisfaction is the most important aspect of customer service, it's important to be able to elaborate on other important techniques in customer service situations. Explain why customer service is such a key part of business, and be sure to expand on the aspect that you deem to be the most important in a way that is reasoned and well-thought out.

59: Is it best to create low or high expectations for a customer?
Answer:
You may answer this question either way (after, of course, determining that the company does not have a clear opinion on the matter). However, no matter which way you answer the question, you must display a thorough thought process, and very clear reasoning for the option you chose. Offer pros and cons of each, and include the ultimate point that tips the scale in favor of your chosen answer.

60: Why did you choose your college major?
Answer:
It's important to display interest in your work, and if your major is related to your current field, it will be simple for you to relate the

two. Perhaps you even knew while in college that you wanted to do a job similar to this position, and so you chose the major so as to receive the education and training you needed to succeed. If your major doesn't relate clearly, it's still important to express a sense of passion for your choice, and to specify the importance of pursuing something that matters to you – which is how you made the decision to come to your current career field instead.

61: Tell me about your college experience.

Answer:

It's best to keep this answer positive – don't focus on parties, pizza, or procrastinating. Instead, offer a general summary of the benefits you received in college, followed by an anecdote of a favorite professor or course that opened up your way of thinking about the field you're in. This is a great opportunity for you to show your passion for your career, make sure to answer enthusiastically and confidently.

62: What is the most unique thing about yourself that you would bring to this position?

Answer:

This question is often asked as a close to an interview, and it gives you a final chance to highlight your best qualities to the employer. Treat the question like a sort of review, and explain why your specific mix of education, experience, and passions will be the ideal combination for the employer. Remain confident but humble, and keep your answer to about two minutes.

63: How did your last job stand up to your previous expectations of it?

Answer:

While it's okay to discuss what you learned if you expected too much out of a previous job, it's best to keep this question away from negative statements or portrayals. Focus your answer around what your previous job did hold that you had expected, and how much you enjoyed those aspects of the position.

64: How did you become interested in this field?

Answer:

This is the chance for you to show your passion for your career – and the interviewer will be assured that you are a great candidate if it's obvious that you enjoy your job. You can include a brief anecdote here in order to make your interest personal, but be sure that it is brief. Offer specific names of mentors or professors who aided in your discovery, and make it clear that you love what you do.

65: What was the greatest thing you learned while in school?

Answer:

By offering a lesson you learned outside of the classroom, you can show the interviewer your capacity for creativity, learning, and reflection. The practical lessons you learned in the classroom are certainly invaluable in their own right and may pertain closely to the position, but showing the mastery of a concept that you had to learn on your own will highlight your growth potential.

66: Tell me about a time when you had to learn a different skill set for a new position.

Answer:

Use a specific example to describe what you had to learn and how you set about outlining goals and tasks for yourself. It's important to show that you mastered the skill largely from your dedication to learning it, and because of the systematic approach you took to developing and honing your individual education. Additionally, draw connections between the skill you learned and the new position, and show how well prepared you are for the job.

67: Tell me about a person who has been a great influence in your career.

Answer:

It's important to make this answer easy to relate to – your story should remind the interviewer of the person who was most influential in his or her own career. Explain what you learned from this person and why they inspired you, and how you hope to model them later in your career with future successes.

68: What would this person tell me about you?

Answer:

Most importantly, if this person is one of your references –they had better know who you are! There are all too many horror stories of professors or past employers being called for a reference, and not being able to recall when they knew you or why you were remarkable, which doesn't send a very positive message to potential employers. This person should remember you as being enthusiastic, passionate, and motivated to learn and succeed.

69: What is the most productive time of day for you?

Answer:

This is a trick question – you should be equally productive all day! While it's normal to become extra motivated for certain projects, and also true that some tasks will require additional work, be sure to emphasize to the interviewer that working diligently throughout the entirety of the day comes naturally to you.

70: What was the most responsibility you were given at your previous job?

Answer:

This question provides you with an opportunity to elaborate on responsibilities that may or may not be on your resume. For instance, your resume may not have allowed room to discuss individual projects you worked on that were really outside the scope of your job responsibilities, but you can tell the interviewer here about the additional work you did and how it translated into new skills and a richer career experience for you.

71: Do you believe you were compensated fairly at your last job?

Answer:

Remember to stay positive, and to avoid making negative comments about your previous employer. If you were not compensated fairly, simply state that you believe your qualities and experience were outside the compensation limitations of the old job, and that you're looking forward to an opportunity that is more in line with the place you're at in your career.

72: Tell me about a time when you received feedback on your work, and enacted it.

Answer:

Try to give an example of feedback your received early in your career, and the steps you took to incorporate it with your work. The most important part of this question is to display the way you learned from the feedback, as well as your willingness to accept suggestions from your superiors. Be sure to offer reflection and understanding of how the feedback helped your work to improve.

73: Tell me about a time when you received feedback on your work that you did not agree with, or thought was unfair. How did you handle it?

Answer:

When explaining that you did not agree with particular feedback or felt it was unfair, you'll need to justify tactfully why the feedback was inaccurate. Then, explain how you communicated directly with the person who offered the feedback, and, most importantly, how you listened to their response, analyzed it, and then came to a mutual agreement.

74: What was your favorite job, and why?

Answer:

It's best if your favorite job relates to the position you're currently applying for, as you can then easily draw connections between why you enjoyed that job and why you are interested in the current position. Additionally, it is extremely important to explain why you've qualified the particular job as your favorite, and what aspects of it you would look for in another job, so that the interviewer can determine whether or not you are a good fit.

75: Tell me about an opportunity that your last position did not allow you to achieve.

Answer:

Stay focused on the positive, and be understanding of the limitations of your previous position. Give a specific example of a goal or career objective that you were not able to achieve, but rather than expressing disappointment over the missed opportunity, discuss the ways you're looking forward to the chance to grow in a new position.

76: Tell me about the worst boss you ever had.

Answer:

It's important to keep this answer brief, and positively focused. While you may offer a couple of short, critical assessments of your boss, focus on the things you learned from working with such an individual, and remain sympathetic to challenges the boss may have faced.

And Finally Good Luck!

INDEX

SQL Server Interview Questions

Engine Enhancements

20: Explain the partition support enhancements in SQL Server.

21: How can SQL Server achieve maximum scalability?

22: What are the additional features included in SQL Server Management Studio?

23: What is the use of Contained Databases?

24: What is the use of FileTable?

25: Explain Full Text search enhancement.

26: What are the editions of SQL Server 2012?

27: What is an in-place upgrade?

28: What are the benefits of side-by-side migration over an in-place upgrade?

29: What are the high level steps performed for Step-by-Step migration?

30: What are the advantages of In-Place upgrade in SQL Server?

Availability and Disaster Recovery Enhancements

31:Explain the Availability modes supported by SQL Server

32: What do you know about the Always On Availability Groups in SQL Server?

33: Explain Failover in AlwaysOn

34: How do you design a backup and recovery solution to the SQL Server database?

35: What is the strategy used for high availability and disaster recovery with SQL server versions prior to 2012?

36: What is the issue with Database mirroring?

37: What is the issue with Log shipping?

38: What are the new features for high availability and disaster recovery introduced in SQL Server 2012?

39: What are the high level benefits of AlwaysOn Availability Groups?

40: What are the high level benefits of AlwaysOn Failover Cluster Instances?

Columnstore Index

64: What is the most important benefit of columnstore index?

65: How many columnstore indexes can be created for a table? Explain with an example.

66: How is data stored in a database using columnstore index?

67: What data types are supported by columnstore index?

68: How does data appear in the table when you use columnstore format?

69: What data types are not supported by columnstore index?

70: How does columnstore index improve the query speed?

71: Explain Batch-mode processing.

72: Explain about segments in columnstore index.

73: What are the restrictions in columnstore index?

74: Which statements are not allowed when you use columnstore index?

75: When should a columnstore index be created?

76: When should a columnstore index not be created?

77: What are the options for loading new data in a columnstore index table?

78: How is new data loaded by using partitioning?

79: How is existing data updated by using partitioning?

80: What tools are used to create columnstore index?

81: Explain the steps to be performed to create columnstore index using Management Studio.

82: How is a clustered columnstore index created?

83: How many columns in a table are supported for columnstore index?

84: Write a query that will force ignore the columnstore index.

85: Write a query that will manually trigger a particular columnstore index.

86: Is it possible to have a clustered B-tree index and non-clustered columnstore index in a table? If so, how will the clustered index be queried?

87: What are the best practices to be followed using columnstore index?

Security Enhancements

88: Explain the Guest User Account in SQL Server

89: Explain the BUILTIN/Administrators Group in SQL Server. What happens when I drop the BUILTIN/Administrators Group?

90: Explain SQL Injection. How can it be handled and prevented?

91: How can you enforce security in SQL Server?

92: What were the improvements introduced in SQL Server 2012 for maximum security and control of DB?

93: What were the security manageability improvements introduced with SQL Server 2012?

94: What is the primary benefit of user-defined server roles?

95: What are the available approaches to creating server roles in SQL Server?

96: What are the steps required to create server roles in SSMS?

97: How will you create server roles using Transact-SQL?

98: How will you define schema?

99: Explain Default Schema for Groups.

100: Where are audit enhancements?

101 :What is an extended event?

102: Write a query that creates a DB and creates schema and tables in that DB.

103: What is the benefit of Record Filtering?

104: Write a query that will create the DB audit specification in myNewschema.

105: What are the common features supported for audit and compliance needs?

106: What are the steps to perform to enable contained DB authentication in Management studio?

107: What are the steps to perform to enable contained DB authentication with Transact-SQL?

108: What are the alternatives for Audit log failure?

109: What are the enhancements to improve resilience other than audit log failures?

110: Write a query to create audit with Fail Operation.

111: What is the benefit of a user-defined audit event?

112: How is a user authenticated against a DB without a login that resides in the engine?

113: What are the benefits of contained database?

114: Use a query to create a contained database user with a password.

115: Use a query to create a contained database user with a domain login.

116: What are the security concerns of contained DB authentication?

Programmability and Beyond-Relational Enhancements

117: What is Beyond Relational in SQL Server?

118: What are the components of Beyond Relational?

119: Explain the special data types hierarchyid, bit, sql_variant, table, sysname, alias and timestamp data types

120: Can you use a user-defined data type created in one database in another database.

121: What does beyond-relational enhancement mean?

122: What are the new beyond-relational enhancements features introduced in SQL Server 2012?

123: Explain File Stream.

124: What are the new File Stream enhancements in SQL Server 2012?

125: Explain beyond-relational features by using an example.

126: Explain RBS.

127: What are the limitations of RBS?

128: What is a FileTable?

129: What are the prerequisites for FileTable?

130: What are the steps to be performed to enable FILESTREAM?

131: How are enable directory and non-transactional access for FileTable accomplished?

Integration Services

153: Explain Scripting Engine.

154: How are Expression Indicators used in Integration Services?

155: Explain the new Undo and Redo feature in SSDT.

156: Explain SQL Server Integration Services Control Flow.

157: Explain SQL Server Integration Services Data Flow.

158: What are the default control flow tasks in SSIS?

159: What are the new tasks added to Control Flow in SSIS?

160: Explain Expression Task in SSIS.

161: Explain Execute Package Task.

162: What are the new features introduced in Execute Package Task in SSIS 2012?

163: What is deployment model?

164: What are the deployment models supported in SSIS?

165: What is Project Deployment Workflow?

166: What are the stages of Project Deployment workflow?

167: What properties are used to configure project parameters?

168: What are execution parameter values?

169: What is Integration Services Catalog?

170: What is the use of encryption in SSIS?

171: What are the various encryptions supported in SSIS?

172: What is environment reference? What are its types?

173: What are the monitoring or troubleshooting tools available in SSIS?

174: Describe the security of Integration Services.

Data Quality Services

175: What are SQL Server's Data Quality Service? Explain briefly the different DQS processes

176: How can DQS help in a Business?

177: What are Reference Data Services in DQS?

178: What happens during DQS profiling and notification?

179: Explain the function Data Quality Services.

180: What features of DQS are used to resolve data quality issue?

181: What are the components of DQS?

182: What databases are installed during installation of Data Quality Server?

183: What roles must be mapped for each user before using DQS_MAIN database?

184: What are the tasks available in Data Quality Client?

185: Explain Knowledge Base Management.

186: What activities are performed using Knowledge base?

187: When you create a new domain for a knowledge base, what are the properties that need to be configured?

188: What are the types of settings to configure for domain value?

189: Explain RDS.

190: How is reference data used to cleanse data?

191: What is the need for a matching policy?

192: What are the steps involved when creating a cleansing data quality project?

193: Explain Matching Projects.

194: What are the steps involved in a matching data quality project?

195: What are the export options available for exporting contents in matching data quality project?

196: What are the steps an Administrator can perform using the features of Data Quality Client?

197: What details can be monitored in the Data Quality Client?

198: What are the pages that can be exported from Data Quality Client monitoring?

199: Explain Data Quality Client configuration.

200: Explain Interactive Cleansing and Profiler setting in Data Quality Client configuration.

201: Where can one subscribe to reference data?

202: Explain DQS in Integration Services.

203: Explain DQS in Master Data services.

Master Data Services

204: What is SQL Master Data Services? Why is it required?

205:Explain the steps involved in creating and deploying an MDS

206: Explain how to deploy an MDS model

207: How do you make sure the master data is secure?

208: What are the core features of the Master Data Services in SQL Server?

209: What are the new improvements of Master Data Services in SQL Server 2012?

210: How is MDS installed or upgraded in SQL Server 2012?

211: Explain the Master Data Manager in MDS.

212: How an Entity Member is managed in MDS?

213: What is the new improvement in SQL Server 2012 MDS for many-to-many relationships?

214: What is Collection Management and how it is handled in MDS?

215: Explain the staging process steps involved in master data management process.

216: What approaches are available to start a staging process in MDS?

217: What are the parameters associated with the staging process execution stored procedure?

218: How User and Group permissions are managed in MDS?

219: What are the tools available for Model Deployment?

220: What is the syntax to run the MDSModelDeploy tool in MDS?

22: What is MDS Add-in for Excel?

222: Explain more about Master data management using Add-in for Excel.

223: Explain the behavior of the MDS Add-in for Excel on data refresh.

224: How is Data Publication done through the Excel worksheet?

225: Discuss elaborately about model building in MDS using Add-in for Excel.

226: What are the Domain-based attributes in a worksheet?

227: What is a shortcut query file in MDS?

228: How Data Quality Services can be used in MDS?

229: Explain the Data-Quality Matching Process in MDS worksheet.

230: How MDS has been integrated with SharePoint?

231: Explain about Bulk Updates and Export in MDS.

232: How are Transactions being used in MDS?

Analysis Services and PowerPivot

233:Differentiate between OLAP and OLTP. Is SQL Server Analysis Services (SSAS) the OLAP or OLTP component of SQL?

234: Which are the Storage Modes that Cube Partitions support?

235: Explain the different aggregation functions available in SSAS

236: What are translations? What is its significance in SSAS?

237: What are the different server modes in which SQL Server 2012 Analysis Services can execute?

238: What type of security is being followed in the different Analysis Services server modes?

239: Name some of the Model Design Features that exist across all the server modes of Analysis Services.

240: How is an analysis services project in SQL Server 2012 created?

241: How many templates are available for Analysis Services Projects and what are they?

242: What is a tabular model in SQL Server 2012?

243: What are the workspace database properties in Model Designer of SQL Server Data Tool?

244: Explain the Tabular Model Designer.

245: How are table relationships managed in model designer?

246: What is a calculated column in analysis service?

247: Explain the Key Performance Indicators in Analysis service.

248: What are the different security permission roles available in the tabular model to perform an action?

249: What are the reporting properties that can be changed on a selected table or column in Model Designer?

250: Compare the model behavior for different available features in In-memory and Direct-Query modes.

251: What are the new features of the Multidimensional model storage in SQL Server 2012 Analysis Services?

252: Explain Event tracing in Analysis Services.

253: What are XMLA Schema Rowsets?

254: What configurations need to be specified to deploy an Analysis Services instances in NUMA architecture?

255: What is PowerPivot for Excel and what are its benefits?

256: What is PowerPivot for SharePoint and what are its benefits?

257: Describe the installation and configuration dependencies associated with PowerPivot for SharePoint.

258: What are the properties required to manage the cache in Management Dashboard?

259: What are the settings associated with health rules of Analysis Services and what are its default values?

260: What is a Data Refresh configuration in Analysis Services?

261: What are the Analysis services functionalities that have been discontinued in SQL Server 2012?

Reporting Services

262: Explain the SQL Server Reporting Services and its components.

263: List out the advantages of using SSRS

264: List out the limitations in the SQL Server express edition of SSRS?

265: What are the Types of SSRS?

266: What are the core features of the Reporting Services in SQL Server from its inception?

267: What are the improvements available in SQL Server 2012 reporting services?

268: What are the new renderers added to SQL Server 2012 reporting services?

269: What are the benefits of the new SharePoint Shared service architecture in SQL Server 2012 reporting services?

270: Explain the Service Application Configuration.

271: What is a Power View?

272: What are the data source types available with Power View?

273: What are the options available to open a Power View Design environment for creating a new report?

274: Explain the Power View Design environment.

275: How are tabular model field lists represented in the Reporting Service Power View design environment?

276: What Data Visualization is available in Power View?

277: Explain about the different types of Chart Visualizations.

278: How to work with overlapping visualizations in Charts?

279: Explain more about Card visualization in Charts.

280: What is a Tile Visualization in Charts?

281: How is play axis used in Scatter chart and Bubble chart?

282: What is "Multiples" in Charts?

283: Elaborate on Power View Filter.

284: What are the display modes available in Power View?

285: How are created reports exported in Power View?

286: What are the features of Data Alerts?

287: What is the process followed for Data Alert Creation?

288: How does the Alerting service process the data alerts?

289: What are the Alert configuration settings and their default values?

290: What are the Alert Service events that are supported for all alerts?

HR Questions

1: How would you handle a negative coworker?

2: What would you do if you witnessed a coworker surfing the web, reading a book, etc, wasting company time?

3: How do you handle competition among yourself and other employees?

4: When is it okay to socialize with coworkers?

5: Tell me about a time when a major change was made at your last job, and how you handled it.

6: When delegating tasks, how do you choose which tasks go to which team members?

7: Tell me about a time when you had to stand up for something you believed strongly about to coworkers or a supervisor.

8: Tell me about a time when you helped someone finish their work, even though it wasn't "your job."

9: What are the challenges of working on a team? How do you handle this?

10: Do you value diversity in the workplace?

11: How would you handle a situation in which a coworker was not accepting of someone else's diversity?

12: Are you rewarded more from working on a team, or accomplishing a task on your own?

13: Tell me about a time when you didn't meet a deadline.

14: How do you eliminate distractions while working?

15: Tell me about a time when you worked in a position with a weekly or monthly quota to meet. How often?

16: Tell me about a time when you met a tough deadline, and how you were able to complete it.

17: How do you stay organized when you have multiple

18: How much time during your work day do you spend on "auto-pilot?"

19: How do you handle deadlines?

20: Tell me about your personal problem-solving process.

47: What is your greatest goal in life?

48: Tell me about a time when you set a goal in your personal life and achieved it.

49: What is your greatest goal in your career?

50: Tell me about a time when you achieved a goal.

51: What areas of your work would you still like to improve in? What are your plans to do this?

52: What is customer service?

53: Tell me about a time when you went out of your way for a customer.

54: How do you gain confidence from customers?

55: Tell me about a time when a customer was upset or agitated – how did you handle the situation?

56: When can you make an exception for a customer?

57: What would you do in a situation where you were needed by both a customer and your boss?

58: What is the most important aspect of customer service?

59: Is it best to create low or high expectations for a customer?

60: Why did you choose your college major?

61: Tell me about your college experience.

62: What is the most unique thing about yourself that you would bring to this position?

63: How did your last job stand up to your previous expectations of it?

64: How did you become interested in this field?

65: What was the greatest thing you learned while in school?

66: Tell me about a time when you had to learn a different skill set for a new position.

67: Tell me about a person who has been a great influence in your career.

68: What would this person tell me about you?

69: What is the most productive time of day for you?

70: What was the most responsibility you were given at your previous job?

71: Do you believe you were compensated fairly at your last job?

72: Tell me about a time when you received feedback on your work, and enacted it.

73: Tell me about a time when you received feedback on your work that you did not agree with, or thought was unfair. How did you handle it?

74: What was your favorite job, and why?

75: Tell me about an opportunity that your last position did not allow you to achieve.

76: Tell me about the worst boss you ever had.

Some of the following titles might also be handy:

1. .NET Interview Questions You'll Most Likely Be Asked
2. 200 Interview Questions You'll Most Likely Be Asked
3. Access VBA Programming Interview Questions You'll Most Likely Be Asked
4. Adobe ColdFusion Interview Questions You'll Most Likely Be Asked
5. Advanced Excel Interview Questions You'll Most Likely Be Asked
6. Advanced JAVA Interview Questions You'll Most Likely Be Asked
7. Advanced SAS Interview Questions You'll Most Likely Be Asked
8. AJAX Interview Questions You'll Most Likely Be Asked
9. Algorithms Interview Questions You'll Most Likely Be Asked
10. Android Development Interview Questions You'll Most Likely Be Asked
11. Ant & Maven Interview Questions You'll Most Likely Be Asked
12. Apache Web Server Interview Questions You'll Most Likely Be Asked
13. Artificial Intelligence Interview Questions You'll Most Likely Be Asked
14. ASP.NET Interview Questions You'll Most Likely Be Asked
15. Automated Software Testing Interview Questions You'll Most Likely Be Asked
16. Base SAS Interview Questions You'll Most Likely Be Asked
17. BEA WebLogic Server Interview Questions You'll Most Likely Be Asked
18. C & C++ Interview Questions You'll Most Likely Be Asked
19. C# Interview Questions You'll Most Likely Be Asked
20. C++ Internals Interview Questions You'll Most Likely Be Asked
21. CCNA Interview Questions You'll Most Likely Be Asked
22. Cloud Computing Interview Questions You'll Most Likely Be Asked
23. Computer Architecture Interview Questions You'll Most Likely Be Asked
24. Computer Networks Interview Questions You'll Most Likely Be Asked
25. Core JAVA Interview Questions You'll Most Likely Be Asked
26. Data Structures & Algorithms Interview Questions You'll Most Likely Be Asked
27. Data WareHousing Interview Questions You'll Most Likely Be Asked
28. EJB 3.0 Interview Questions You'll Most Likely Be Asked
29. Entity Framework Interview Questions You'll Most Likely Be Asked
30. Fedora & RHEL Interview Questions You'll Most Likely Be Asked
31. GNU Development Interview Questions You'll Most Likely Be Asked
32. Hibernate, Spring & Struts Interview Questions You'll Most Likely Be Asked
33. HTML, XHTML and CSS Interview Questions You'll Most Likely Be Asked
34. HTML5 Interview Questions You'll Most Likely Be Asked
35. IBM WebSphere Application Server Interview Questions You'll Most Likely Be Asked
36. iOS SDK Interview Questions You'll Most Likely Be Asked
37. Java / J2EE Design Patterns Interview Questions You'll Most Likely Be Asked
38. Java / J2EE Interview Questions You'll Most Likely Be Asked
39. Java Messaging Service Interview Questions You'll Most Likely Be Asked
40. JavaScript Interview Questions You'll Most Likely Be Asked
41. JavaServer Faces Interview Questions You'll Most Likely Be Asked
42. JDBC Interview Questions You'll Most Likely Be Asked
43. jQuery Interview Questions You'll Most Likely Be Asked
44. JSP-Servlet Interview Questions You'll Most Likely Be Asked
45. JUnit Interview Questions You'll Most Likely Be Asked
46. Linux Commands Interview Questions You'll Most Likely Be Asked
47. Linux Interview Questions You'll Most Likely Be Asked
48. Linux System Administrator Interview Questions You'll Most Likely Be Asked
49. Mac OS X Lion Interview Questions You'll Most Likely Be Asked
50. Mac OS X Snow Leopard Interview Questions You'll Most Likely Be Asked

51. Microsoft Access Interview Questions You'll Most Likely Be Asked
52. Microsoft Excel Interview Questions You'll Most Likely Be Asked
53. Microsoft Powerpoint Interview Questions You'll Most Likely Be Asked
54. Microsoft Word Interview Questions You'll Most Likely Be Asked
55. MySQL Interview Questions You'll Most Likely Be Asked
56. NetSuite Interview Questions You'll Most Likely Be Asked
57. Networking Interview Questions You'll Most Likely Be Asked
58. OOPS Interview Questions You'll Most Likely Be Asked
59. Operating Systems Interview Questions You'll Most Likely Be Asked
60. Oracle DBA Interview Questions You'll Most Likely Be Asked
61. Oracle E-Business Suite Interview Questions You'll Most Likely Be Asked
62. ORACLE PL/SQL Interview Questions You'll Most Likely Be Asked
63. Perl Programming Interview Questions You'll Most Likely Be Asked
64. PHP Interview Questions You'll Most Likely Be Asked
65. PMP Interview Questions You'll Most Likely Be Asked
66. Python Interview Questions You'll Most Likely Be Asked
67. RESTful JAVA Web Services Interview Questions You'll Most Likely Be Asked
68. Ruby Interview Questions You'll Most Likely Be Asked
69. Ruby on Rails Interview Questions You'll Most Likely Be Asked
70. SAP ABAP Interview Questions You'll Most Likely Be Asked
71. SAP HANA Interview Questions You'll Most Likely Be Asked
72. SAS Programming Guidelines Interview Questions You'll Most Likely Be Asked
73. Selenium Testing Tools Interview Questions You'll Most Likely Be Asked
74. Silverlight Interview Questions You'll Most Likely Be Asked
75. Software Repositories Interview Questions You'll Most Likely Be Asked
76. Software Testing Interview Questions You'll Most Likely Be Asked
77. SQL Server Interview Questions You'll Most Likely Be Asked
78. Tomcat Interview Questions You'll Most Likely Be Asked
79. UML Interview Questions You'll Most Likely Be Asked
80. Unix Interview Questions You'll Most Likely Be Asked
81. UNIX Shell Programming Interview Questions You'll Most Likely Be Asked
82. VB.NET Interview Questions You'll Most Likely Be Asked
83. Windows Server 2008 R2 Interview Questions You'll Most Likely Be Asked
84. XLXP, XSLT, XPATH, XFORMS & XQuery Interview Questions You'll Most Likely Be Asked
85. XML Interview Questions You'll Most Likely Be Asked

For complete list visit

www.vibrantpublishers.com

NOTES

www.ingramcontent.com/pod-product-compliance
Lightning Source LLC
Chambersburg PA
CBHW071244050326
40690CB00011B/2259

* 9 7 8 1 9 4 6 3 8 3 0 4 4 *